RUN FOR SOMETHING

RUN FOR SOMETHING

A Real-Talk Guide to Fixing the System Yourself

AMANDA LITMAN

ATRIA PAPERBACK

New York   London   Toronto   Sydney   New Delhi

To my 2012, 2014, and 2016 campaign families.
You are all my Fight Song.

An Imprint of Simon & Schuster, Inc.
1230 Avenue of the Americas
New York, NY 10020

First Atria Paperback edition October 2017

ATRIA PAPERBACK and colophon are trademarks of Simon & Schuster, Inc.

For information about special discounts for bulk purchases, please contact Simon & Schuster Special Sales at 1-866-506-1949 or business@simonandschuster.com.

The Simon & Schuster Speakers Bureau can bring authors to your live event. For more information or to book an event, contact the Simon & Schuster Speakers Bureau at 1-866-248-3049 or visit our website at www.simonspeakers.com.

Interior design by Jason Snyder

Manufactured in the United States of America

10 9 8 7 6 5 4 3 2 1

Library of Congress Cataloging-in-Publication Data is available.

ISBN 978-1-5011-8044-6
ISBN 978-1-5011-8045-3 (ebook)

CONTENTS

INTRODUCTION: WHY I WROTE THIS BOOK vii

What's the Worst that Could Happen? by Secretary Hillary Rodham Clinton 1

1 **WHY YOU HAVE TO RUN FOR OFFICE** 5

A Pep Talk by Emmy Ruiz 22

2 **WHY WINNING ISN'T EVERYTHING** (OR, AN EXCUSE TO TALK ABOUT THE UTTER BULLSHIT THAT IS THE UNCONTESTED ELECTION) 27

3 **CIVICS 101: HOW GOVERNMENT (GENERALLY) WORKS AT THE FEDERAL AND STATE LEVELS** (OR, WHY YOU SHOULD RUN FOR LOCAL OFFICE) 35

4 **WHY YOU CAN ACTUALLY RUN FOR STATE LEGISLATURE** 49

Running as a Progressive in a Red State by Jason Kander 62

Do Something by Senator Cory Booker 65

5 **HOW TO RUN FOR OFFICE** 69

Running a Campaign: Tips from an Expert by Jen O'Malley Dillon 90

6 **MOBILIZATION** (OR, HOW YOU REACH VOTERS) 95

7 **MESSAGE** (OR, WHAT YOU TALK TO VOTERS ABOUT) 129

8 **MONEY** (OR, HOW TO RAISE WHAT YOU NEED) 141

9 **WRITING YOUR CAMPAIGN PLAN** 155

Make Local Elections Great Again by Addisu Demissie 163

10 **SO YOU'RE NOT RUNNING FOR OFFICE** (YET) 167

Seven Questions with John Podesta 178

11 **WHY I MADE CAMPAIGNS A CAREER** (AND WHY YOU SHOULD TOO) 181

Campaigns Will Change Your Life by Marlon Marshall 189

Politics Isn't Broken by Teddy Goff 192

12 **HOW TO ACTUALLY GET A JOB ON A POLITICAL CAMPAIGN** 195

13 **PHONE CALLS AND TWEETING AND MARCHING, OH MY** (OR, ACTIVISM 101) 201

CONCLUSION 205

APPENDIX 207 ACKNOWLEDGMENTS 215 NOTES 220

INTRODUCTION
Why I Wrote This Book

■ **I'm not an inspirational speaker** or a motivational writer—this isn't a self-help book. I'm a campaign hack, a political junkie, and a workaholic.

I was born and raised in Fairfax, Virginia. I always knew I wanted to work in politics—I knocked on doors for senatorial and gubernatorial campaigns as a teenager. I was obsessed with *The West Wing* and read the *Washington Post* every morning over breakfast. In high school, I took my first-ever skip day in 2007 to see Barack Obama speak at the university nearby before he even announced he was running. (I was, and might still be, a little bit insufferable.)

I chose Northwestern University in Evanston, Illinois, for college in no small part because I hoped Obama would win, I hoped he would run again, and I hoped he would run his reelection campaign out of Chicago so I could intern for him. Throughout college, I worked at my local Democratic committee, on Capitol Hill, and at political magazines. I majored in American studies, focusing on gender and politics. My senior year, I got a job interning on the digital team for Obama 2012. They hired me a month before I graduated. When I took a day off to walk at graduation, I spent the ceremony answering emails on my phone, which I'd hidden in my gown.

After the campaign ended (reminder: we won!), I helped launch Organizing for Action, the president's nonprofit, as deputy email director. My team helped to raise $26 million online in the first year—a third of the organization's operating budget—and defined what the organization stood for.

I left OFA in March 2014 to work as the digital director for Charlie Crist's gubernatorial campaign in Florida. I raised $2 million, created a groundbreaking tool to help Floridians vote by mail, almost got charged with ten thousand counts of voter fraud (but, for the record, I didn't!), and served as senior staff on the biggest gubernatorial race in the country that year. We lost by just a hair over 1 percent after our opponent, Governor Rick Scott, spent $13 million of his own money on TV in the final two weeks leading up to Election Day.

I then took six weeks to drink and sleep, and in January 2015, I started working for what would become Hillary Clinton's 2016 presidential campaign. As her email director, I managed a nineteen-person team of incredible writers and strategists to help raise more than $330 million online, recruit half a million volunteers, and run the most profitable Democratic store ever. I was younger than nearly all my peers and half the people I managed. I worked 100-hour weeks for two years straight, ruined my personal life, lost an election, and gained a family. Even with the result and even with the day-to-day misery, I don't regret a single minute of it. (More on that on page 181.)

After we lost, I became—and remain—so damn angry.

My anger is indiscriminate. I'm angry at the institutions that have failed me. I'm angry at the people who didn't believe elections matter. I'm angry at the people who made some kind of false equivalence between Donald Trump and Hillary Clinton, and I'm angry at the media coverage that enabled it. I'm angry at the old white men in government who think they understand my problems as a twentysomething woman in America but have never had to deal with paying for an IUD or negotiate for equal pay at a job—and don't get me started on the ones who still have to be taught how to check their own email. I'm angry at a system that makes it so hard to run for office and at a party that perpetually encouraged rich lawyers to run and then seems shocked to find itself without a diverse pipeline of talent.

But very little angers me more than people who complain endlessly without offering solutions or trying to fix the problem. So, after another few weeks of drinking and sleeping, I decided to solve at least one thing myself: I could help young people run for office and rebuild the Democratic bench in the process. I rationalized my decision to myself and others: I'm unemployed, I know politics, I know how the internet works, and I've got the rage-fueled energy to do the work. At the very least, I could turn this into a fun hobby while I got a real job.

I partnered with a cofounder, Ross Morales Rocketto, a friend with a decade of campaign management experience, and we found a group of advisors who'd stand by us.

On January 20, 2017, Inauguration Day, we launched Run for Something, a political action committee dedicated to helping young people run for office by lowering the barriers to entry. We launched a website, opened up a bank account, filled out paperwork, and sent a press release to a list of reporters we'd acquired from some friends in PR. Then we emailed our friends, posted on Facebook, and crossed our fingers.

The immediate reaction was astounding. Thousands and thousands of people signed up to say they wanted to run for office. Volunteers started dedicating hours of their weeks to talk to people about running. Hundreds of Obama, Clinton, and Bernie Sanders campaign alumni joined folks from across the progressive movement to mentor our candidates for free. We're supporting our candidates with resources and funding—and already it's making a difference in school board, city council, and state legislative races across the country.

Our goal is to change the landscape of the world by planting a whole lot of seeds in the form of young progressive candidates. I hope this book can help.

———————

But I don't want to sugarcoat this: Running for office is really fucking hard.

You'll be worried about money all the time. You'll have to make tough decisions, and each choice you make will be dissected. People will dig up your old tweets and cite them in articles. You'll be a little lonely. You'll spend hours and hours every day asking for money and votes. If you do it right, you'll wear out your shoes knocking on doors. If you don't have unlimited data on your cell phone plan, watch out.

You don't get a day off on the campaign trail. You might have to quit your job. Your personal life might go on pause until Election Day. You might not sleep. You'll be living off old coffee and pizza.

And you'll probably lose. (After all, incumbents win 90 percent of the time).

Winning isn't necessarily easy, either. You'll have to get right to work representing your constituents and keeping the promises you made during the campaign, plus you'll likely immediately have to start working for your next election. You'll have to balance short-term and long-term priorities, you'll have to learn about policy issues you might never have encountered before, you probably won't make much money, and you'll spend a lot of time on stuff that's really important—but you'll get zero credit for it. You'll deal with donors, press, coalitions, and constituency groups, and you'll spend a lot of time in meetings with no results.

Do it anyway. Run for office. Even though it's hard, even though you might lose, and even if you're scared—especially if you're scared—if you care about the future of our country and our democracy, you need to run. You can do this.

You really don't have a choice. Look at the world right now.

As I'm writing this, Donald Trump is president. (Thanks, Vladimir Putin, for that.) In 2017, the Republican Party has total control of twenty-six state governments, runs the legislatures in seven others, and can have its way with the entire federal government.

If these (craven, spineless, shameless) elected officials carry out even some of their promises, we're fucked.

The "party of Lincoln," at any given moment, could take away health care from tens of millions of people (if they haven't already). They could limit access to abortion and health care for women, disenfranchise minority voters, and deport millions. They want to lower taxes for the rich and in the process screw over the same voters who got them into office. At any moment, war seems imminent with at least a half dozen countries. Our public education system suffers while the private-prison industrial complex grows.

Climate change could ensure a sweet early release from this political nightmare since the Republican Party refuses to admit it's a problem and isn't doing anything to slow it down. But before the ice caps totally melt, say goodbye to freedom of the press and hello to a newly emboldened group of racists, anti-Semites, bigots, and white supremacists. The fundamental principles of our democracy have been stomped on and thrown out the window.

————————

So, I ask you: Are you as angry at Congress, at your state legislature, at your party—at everyone—as I am? Are you afraid? Are you burned out?

Did you march with women on January 21, 2017, or show up at airports to fight the Muslim ban? Is protest your new brunch? Do you go to town halls during congressional recess? Do you call your members of Congress every single day to make sure they know where you stand on the issues? Are you complaining, and tweeting, and sharing every last video explainer on what Trump's up to?

Good! Thank you. But that's not enough.

You have to run for office. Or at least, you have to think about it. After all, you can't change the game if you don't change the players.

If you're a Republican, well, I'm not going to talk you out of running. After all, as long as you believe in facts, you're probably not as whackadoodle or extreme as Trump. If you're a Democrat, great—me too—you and I have elected officials who need to be held accountable.

Forget about Congress, though. Focus on the offices that actually get shit done—state legislatures, city councils, school boards, and mayorships. Look at who's leading the resistance: the local officials who truly understand their communities.

There are more than half a million elected offices in the United States. For context: That's a *lot*. There are more elected offices in the country than there are McDonald's employees.

Not-so-fun fact: More than 40 percent of state legislative races in 2016 were uncontested, up from nearly one-third of state legislative races in 2012. (That's infuriating and civically negligent. I could go on about why uncontested elections make my blood boil. In fact, I do: Jump to page 27 for a diatribe about why uncontested elections are a scourge on our democracy.)

Sure, for some of these races, gerrymandering is partially to blame. But not entirely! Many of the candidates in these races go unopposed because our political parties have failed to get more people interested in running. We've made it too damn hard to get in the door by professionalizing campaigns to the point that they are only accessible to rich or well-connected people, adding bureaucratic hurdles to jump over, and failing to provide data or information on anything as basic as what the offices are.

Institutions tend to focus recruitment efforts on "flippable" seats or open races and then recruit for fundraising capability (a heuristic used to assess a candidate's likelihood of winning) instead of authenticity, diversity, or potential—and then in the case of Democrats, find ourselves without a deep bench of talent. The party complains about low turnout but in too many places doesn't give people actual options to vote for!

So, I repeat: You have to run, or at least think about running, especially if you've never thought about running before.

If you're reading this book, you're exactly what most politicians have to pretend to be: a real person.

Think you're not qualified? Let me make something extremely clear: DONALD TRUMP IS PRESIDENT OF THE UNITED STATES. YOU CAN BE A STATE SENATOR. OR ON YOUR CITY COUNCIL. OR ON YOUR SCHOOL BOARD.

I get it—on the one hand, what kind of egotistical nightmare thinks they're qualified to represent hundreds or thousands or tens of thousands of people in government? How entitled must you be to think you can handle the job?

And if you're a woman or a person of color, you're probably second-guessing yourself because you don't see as many people like you who've run and won before. (An aside to women and people of color: Approach this and every decision with the confidence of an entitled, mediocre white man—he'd never even ask himself this kind of question.)

Our elected officials are, by and large, a sea of old white men who don't actually represent the diversity of this country. You have to fix it.

So don't worry about your résumé. Remember: Barack Obama was a community organizer with a funny name before he was a state senator. Patty Murray was a "mom in tennis shoes" before she was a member of the School District Board of Directors, the Washington State Senate, then the United States Senate. If you're smart, if you care, and if you're willing to learn and work hard, you can run and you can serve. If you win, you can hire people to help you with the work.

You don't need to be charismatic. You certainly don't need to be an extrovert. All you need is a good brain and a willingness to work as hard as it takes.

There are a lot of barriers to entry. It's expensive. It's scary. The pay isn't high enough and the work is hard. But you can fix the system by joining it. You can do something with your outrage and your sadness. You can be fearless.

Pardon the cliché, but win or lose, you will actually be the change you wish to see in the world.

You can do it. And this book will help you figure out how.

———————

You be the one in italics, I'll be me:

Well, I've never even thought about running for office.
Until now—you're thinking about it now, right? Most people don't think about it until someone else asks them to think about it.

I don't live in DC.

We need to fill more than half a million positions; 99 percent of them are not in DC.

I didn't study political science.

Me neither. What you study in college has little to no relation on your fitness to run for office and work as a public servant (or, honestly, to most jobs).

I don't have very much money.

That's why you ask people to invest in your campaign.

I have too many embarrassing photos on social media.

Donald Trump is president. Who cares?

I don't think I'm qualified.

Are you smart? Are you a good listener? Are you willing to work really fucking hard? Great. You're qualified to run for office.

I have a family—what would I do with my kids?

Okay, yes, it's going to be harder for you. Your friends and family will have to help you out. But if you're fighting for something righteous, you'd be surprised at what people will do.

I really don't want people blaming me for problems in our town.

Well, that's part of being a public servant: You'll work for your constituents. The flip side of being responsible for the problems is that you'll also be responsible for the solutions too. Your work will matter.

I'm not interested in actually running for office (but maybe I could help other people do so).

Great! Get a sneak peek into what a campaign is like. Then run for office in two years. Or decide that working on campaigns is your new side hustle.

I super don't want to run for office. Stop trying to convince me. I'm not doing it. Leave me alone.

Understanding how campaigns work is important, even if you don't ever want to run. As a voter and a citizen, you should know how your public servants are trying to get your attention.

And for what it's worth, campaigns are interesting as organizational endeavors. Every campaign is a teensy start-up with an expiration date. If you're looking for experience in business or operations or tech or nonprofits, campaigns are worth understanding, both for their flaws and their successes.

Okay. Fine. I'll read the book. Or skim it. What now?

———————

This book is structured like a mix between a *Vox*-style explainer and a Choose Your Own Adventure book. You don't need to read it straight through, and in fact, it might be better if you jump around a bit. Start with the question: Are you thinking about running for office? Then see where you go!

The first chapter is mandatory and answers the question of why you have to run for office right freakin' now.

If you decide not to (or decide to run one day, but not right now), jump to chapter 10, page 167, where I talk about what you can do instead of running, why you should work on campaigns, and why, dear God, you have to vote.

If you decide to run immediately, I'll help you figure out what office to run for with a little Civics 101 refresher, starting on page 35. Then it's off to the races to learn what the fuck a campaign is and how all the pieces work. I'll define terms for you, give you some key words to search for so you can find the resources you need, and include a glossary at the end for anything you might not understand.

This book is about tactics and strategy. No bullshit here—you need to literally know what to do. For example, it's not helpful to be told "set up meetings with key players in the community" when you might not know who the key players are, so I'll try to guide you to the right way to find that kind of information.

Additionally, as a candidate, you'll have limited bandwidth, so I'll identify what the most important thing you need to do is and what the bonus is if you have the cash or capacity.

———————

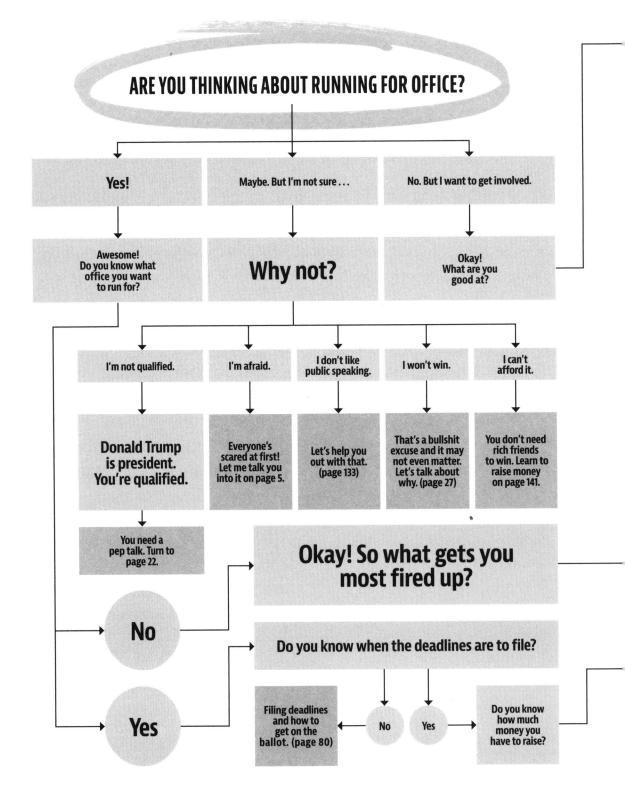

ARE YOU THINKING ABOUT RUNNING FOR OFFICE?

Yes!

Maybe. But I'm not sure . . .

No. But I want to get involved.

Awesome!
Do you know what
office you want
to run for?

Why not?

Okay!
What are you
good at?

I'm not qualified.

I'm afraid.

I don't like
public speaking.

I won't win.

I can't
afford it.

**Donald Trump
is president.
You're qualified.**

Everyone's
scared at first!
Let me talk you
into it on page 5.

Let's help you
out with that.
(page 133)

That's a bullshit
excuse and it may
not even matter.
Let's talk about
why. (page 27)

You don't need
rich friends
to win. Learn to
raise money
on page 141.

You need a
pep talk. Turn to
page 22.

Okay! So what gets you
most fired up?

No

Do you know when the deadlines are to file?

Yes

Filing deadlines
and how to
get on the
ballot. (page 80)

No

Yes

Do you know
how much
money you
have to raise?

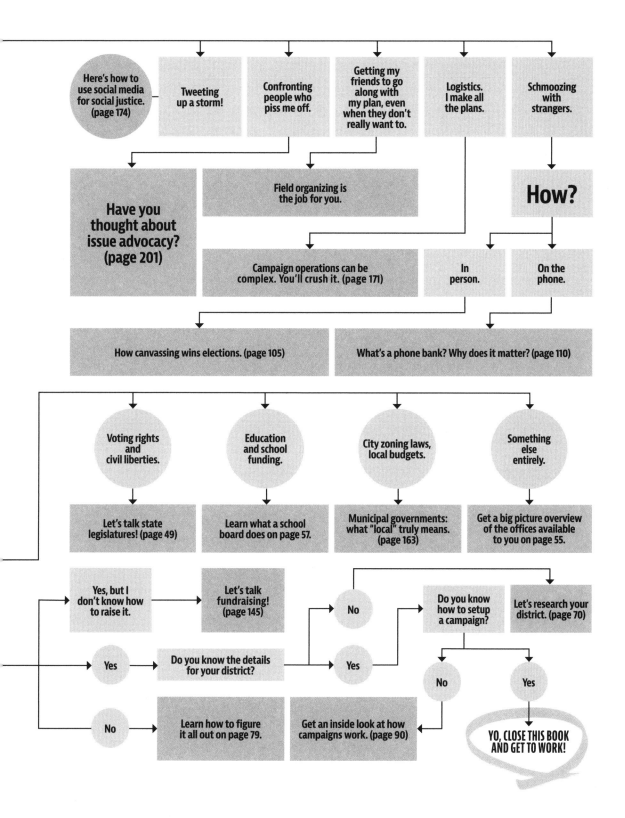

Here's how to use social media for social justice. (page 174)

Tweeting up a storm!

Confronting people who piss me off.

Getting my friends to go along with my plan, even when they don't really want to.

Logistics. I make all the plans.

Schmoozing with strangers.

Have you thought about issue advocacy? (page 201)

Field organizing is the job for you.

How?

Campaign operations can be complex. You'll crush it. (page 171)

In person.

On the phone.

How canvassing wins elections. (page 105)

What's a phone bank? Why does it matter? (page 110)

Voting rights and civil liberties.

Education and school funding.

City zoning laws, local budgets.

Something else entirely.

Let's talk state legislatures! (page 49)

Learn what a school board does on page 57.

Municipal governments: what "local" truly means. (page 163)

Get a big picture overview of the offices available to you on page 55.

Yes, but I don't know how to raise it.

Let's talk fundraising! (page 145)

No

Do you know how to setup a campaign?

Let's research your district. (page 70)

Yes

Do you know the details for your district?

Yes

No

Learn how to figure it all out on page 79.

Get an inside look at how campaigns work. (page 90)

No

Yes

YO, CLOSE THIS BOOK AND GET TO WORK!

A key note here: Campaigns in big cities like Miami or Chicago are a little different from campaigns in, say, rural Kansas or Idaho. So if something here doesn't make sense for your community, ignore it. I'll explain the rationale behind a suggested tactic, so you can figure out how it applies to where you live. I also assume that you've never been involved in politics before. If you know this stuff, breeze right past it.

I'm also just focusing on local races—the usual first entry point for elected officials. Congressional races, statewide races, and the like are much bigger and require more money, more staff, and more resources.

Finally, an editorial note: I'm a progressive, so the guidance and institutional structures referenced in this book come from that part of the political world. I want to help more pro-equality, pro-women, pro-tolerance, pro-immigrant, pro–voting rights people run and win. I hope you're committed to truth and science, to listening to voters, and to governing by putting your values first. To be 100 percent honest, even with all my outrage at the institutional Democratic Party, at the end of the day, I'm still a Democrat, and I want more Democrats to run and win.

You don't have to be one to take my advice, but for all I know Republicans do it totally differently. Move forward (and use this book) at your own risk.

What's the Worst that Could Happen?

by Secretary Hillary Rodham Clinton

Democratic nominee for President of the United States in 2016 | U.S. Secretary of State, 2009–13 | U.S. Senator of New York, 2001–09 | First Lady of the United States, 1993–01

■ **Deciding to run for office** can be an agonizing process—take it from someone who's been there. Back in 1999, there was a lot of speculation that I might run for the Senate. In fact, reading newspapers and listening to folks on TV, it seemed like it was pretty much a done deal—for everyone, that is, except me. Democrats in New York were urging me to run, and I kept telling them no. There were plenty of other people who had been in line a lot longer than I had. My most recent experience as a candidate was for student council. I'd always been an advocate, not a politician. As far as I was concerned, there were a million reasons why it was a terrible idea.

Then one day I went to an event at a school in New York City with young women athletes and Billie Jean King. Hanging over our heads was a giant banner that said "Dare to compete." When it was my turn to speak, a young woman named Sophia introduced me. Sophia was the captain of the girls' basketball team. She was extremely poised and very tall. As I approached the microphone, I reached out to shake her hand and thank her for the introduction. She leaned down and whispered in my ear, "Dare to compete, Mrs. Clinton, dare to compete."

That's when it clicked. For years, I had been telling women to step up and participate, to fight for what they believe in. And yet here I was, holding back. Could it be I was too scared to do what I had urged so many others to do?

What ultimately pushed me to run in the first place was remembering something

I learned when I was a little girl: My family and my faith taught me to do all the good you can, in all the ways you can, for as many people as you can, for as long as you can. Getting off the sidelines and into the arena has given me a chance to solve problems and help people. Despite all the setbacks and disappointments, I wouldn't trade that for anything in the world.

Politics can be a tough business, but it's nothing compared to the struggles millions of people face every day. On tough days, I think about everyone I've met who has inspired me to keep going. People like Ryan Moore, whom I first met as a seven-year-old. He was wearing a full body brace that must have weighed forty pounds, and grinning from ear to ear. Ryan and his family kept me going when our plan for universal health care failed, and kept me working with leaders from both parties to help create the Children's Health Insurance Program. Today, CHIP covers eight million kids every year. Or like Lauren Manning, who was gravely injured on 9/11. It was Lauren, and all the victims and survivors, who spurred me on when I headed to the floor of the Senate on behalf of 9/11 families and first responders who got sick from their time at Ground Zero. I was thinking of Lauren ten years later in the White House Situation Room when President Obama made the courageous decision that finally brought Osama bin Laden to justice. There is nothing more rewarding than knowing your efforts helped make a difference in someone's life.

When I lost the 2016 presidential election, my biggest fear was that the people who supported me—especially the young people—would be discouraged. But over the last several months, I've been energized by the outpouring of grassroots activism and organizing across America—from the Women's Marches to airports across the country where communities are standing with immigrants and refugees to the ongoing fight to protect affordable health care. And I've been particularly inspired by all the women and young people stepping up to run for office—because it means my defeat hasn't defeated them.

That's why I'm so proud of the efforts of groups like Run for Something, and so glad this book exists. I wish I'd had it years ago, and I'm overjoyed that I'll be able to recommend it to aspiring candidates from now on. This book will take you through the basics—like learning about your local party, raising money, and telling people what you stand for. It's also full of great advice from people who really know what they're talking about, including a few of the smart, hardworking staffers I was so fortunate to have as part of my campaign family.

You've probably noticed that this book doesn't pretend running for office will be easy. The pace of a campaign is relentless. As a candidate, you'll have a lot of responsibility on your shoulders. Being a woman candidate can be especially lonely (though if more of us ran, it would be a lot less lonely, wouldn't it?). You'll have to face criticism, both founded and unfounded, about everything from your policies to your appearance. Sometimes the personal attacks can really sting. And yes, you might lose, which is awful. But you get through it—with a little help from family and friends, good books, Netflix, and long walks in the woods.

You don't have to run for president (though I hope at least some of you will give it some serious thought). Change doesn't always come from Washington, D.C. It can come from your local school board or city council. In fact, most of the progress we're seeing right now is happening on the local level. Policy ideas we worked on and fought for during the campaign are taking hold in cities and states across the country—like New York, which recently became the first state in the nation to make public college tuition-free for working families.

Scrolling through Twitter, it's easy to get discouraged and disillusioned—to throw up your hands and decide that our political system is hopelessly broken. But I don't believe that. And if you're reading this book, chances are you don't believe it either.

Everywhere I went on the 2016 campaign, I met people with great ideas. There were passionate activists, and people who were surprised to find themselves advocating for an issue. There were small-business owners who became community leaders, and nurses who were speaking out for affordable health care. There were workers risking their jobs for a living wage, and DREAMers risking everything to stand up for their families. And yes, there were a whole lot of frustrated young people sick of feeling like the people running their country didn't represent them. I told them the same thing I'm telling you now: Run for office. Don't wait for someone else to come along and fight for your community—do it yourself.

The only way we'll ever be able to tackle the challenges we face as a country is if more people get involved. If you've ever obsessed over an issue . . . if you've ever been "that person" talking politics at a party . . . if you've ever worried about the schools your kids go to or the care we provide to our veterans . . . if your student loans are way too high . . . if you think it's unfair that the wealthiest 1 percent of Americans control 99 percent of this country's wealth . . . if you believe, sometimes despite overwhelming chatter to the contrary, that politics can change the world for the better . . . I hope you will think seriously about running for office. After all, what's the worst that could happen? If I could go back, I'd change the outcome, but I wouldn't give back the experiences I had along the way. So enjoy the book, and then go out there and effect change. We really, really need you.

1
WHY YOU HAVE TO RUN FOR OFFICE

■ **No one asked Donald Trump** to run for president.

(Putin might have asked Donald Trump to run for president.)

Why would they? He wasn't qualified. He had a résumé most people would scoff at: he'd filed for bankruptcy many times over, had a record of making racist and sexist remarks, has been married three times, and had racked up an impressive number of sexual misconduct allegations. In short, his last few decades in the spotlight would have embarrassed even his own parents (as if Trump didn't already have daddy issues).

He was literally a joke—the reality TV star was the butt of President Obama's White House Correspondents' Association dinner speech in 2011. No one ever would have said to him: "Donald, it's your time. Run for office! We need you."

But he did. And then Trump won the election. (I'd say fair and square, but the Russians had something to do with it, so let's leave it at he won the electoral college and move on.)

Donald Trump is president of the United States of America. (As of this writing, at least. Who knows what might happen?)

It's likely that, just like Donald, you're not going to be asked to run for office. No one is going to come up and tap you on the shoulder to tell you it's your turn.

Until right now. I'm asking you to run for office.

You can't wait for the cavalry to save the day. You can't wait for someone else to have the courage. Every possible excuse you can come up with is bullshit. If Donald Trump can be our president, even if he's an incompetent one, you can run for local office.

Let's start with a big one: It's okay if you don't look or sound like a politician.

> *When I was knocking on doors I heard whispers and grumblings about me being gay, and I would say, 'Listen, I'm not scared or afraid of my past. Let me be very clear right off the bat: I'm proudly gay, I'm HIV-positive, I'm Puerto Rican, and I'm formerly homeless. This is who I am.' I think these details actually add to the richness of your story and your life. A lot of people out here are struggling and are being marginalized. They want somebody who can relate to them— not somebody from a different stratosphere.*
>
> —NELSON ROMAN, city councilor of Holyoke, MA, on owning his story

Think a little bit about what the expression "look like a politician" means—the image of "politician" probably (and unfortunately) draws to mind an old white dude.

In 2014, Pew Research Center surveyed the adult population and found that approximately 2 percent of Americans have ever run for federal, local, or state office. And according to Pew's "Profile of the 2%," people who seek office tend to be exactly what we picture: white, male, and well-educated.[1]

Because fewer women and fewer people of color run, the number of women and people of color in elected office often doesn't statistically reflect the population served.

Let's start with "WHITE": According to that same Pew study, non-Hispanic whites make up 66 percent of the American adult population but 82 percent of the people who've sought elected office. Non-Hispanic blacks make up 12 percent of the population but only 5 percent of office-seekers. Fifteen percent of U.S. adults are Hispanic, but only 6 percent have run for office.

"MALE": Women make up only a quarter of the people who've run for office and are overwhelmingly underrepresented at all levels of government. The City University of New York Institute for State and Local Governance put out a study in the fall of 2016 that breaks it down.[2]

19.4 percent of the U.S. Congress are women

24.6 percent of U.S. state legislators are women

33.6 percent of city councils in the top 100 U.S. cities are women

18.2 percent of elected mayors in the top 100 U.S. cities are women

19.3 percent of mayoral candidates in the top 100 U.S. cities are women

This isn't our fault. Research shows women are less likely than men to be encouraged by parents, teachers, or party leaders to run—to put a number to it, men are 15 percent more likely to be recruited to run.[3] When women run, we win at the same rates as men, but we're not getting in the door in the first place. (I'll get into who does this "recruiting" later, but if you're impatient to find out, here's a sneak preview: It's often a bunch of men who work at a party committee, who ask their friends to run.)

Women are also less likely to run without being prodded. Countless academic studies show that we underestimate our abilities and assume we need to be even more qualified than men in order to run for office, or apply for that job, or raise our hand to speak. Sound familiar? Every time I read an article that highlights research like this, alarm bells of self-recognition go off in my head. Fuck you, patriarchy.

There are clear systemic problems holding women back: We're often the heads of our households and/or primary caretakers of our kids or parents. We tend to have less disposable income. Still, we can't let the bastards grind us down. The sad reality is that if women are going to be fairly represented in government, more of us will need to make the sacrifice, do the hard work, and run anyway.

Finally, "OLD:" More than 40 percent of adults who have *ever* run for office are sixty-five and older, directly impacting the makeup of our government. Only 5 percent of state legislators are under the age of thirty-five! Even though these legislating bodies are making decisions that affect the under-thirty-five demographic (i.e., me, and maybe you), we're not usually part of the conversation.

That is not to say that old white men don't have value: They do. But they can't be the only ones in the room.

So, unfortunately, if you're a young woman, a young person of color, or anything other than an old white dude, you might not have as many role models, mentors, or networks that make running for office easier.

And on top of that, yes, the bar is higher for you. Mediocre white men get a pass; you don't. That just sucks. But the only way you fix it is by running, winning, and then changing the system to let more people like you in.

Don't second-guess yourself. Put aside your imposter syndrome—even the most extraordinary people assume they're not qualified.

For example: Oprah Winfrey gave an interview after the 2016 election in which she told *Bloomberg*'s David Rubenstein she had always assumed she wasn't qualified to be president. Oprah, the queen and dragon slayer herself, believed she wasn't qualified to serve in public office.

Whether or not I think Oprah is qualified to be president is beside the point—I don't think she should be president.

I think *YOU* should be president. Or your friend, or your sister. You should think about it, at least. And to get there one day, you have to start small. Start local. Donald Trump is president; forget the rules. You can do anything.

It doesn't matter if you live in a red state.

It is certainly going to be harder if you live in a place that voted for Trump by fifty points. But that doesn't mean you shouldn't run. In fact, I think it's even more important that you run.

The way we promote progressive values is through people like you arguing for our policies on a local level in an authentic way, rooted in your community.

Your campaign will galvanize other people like you in your area—if, hypothetically, Trump won your district with 75 percent of the vote, that still means 25 percent of voters are with you. And those 25 percent of voters will see someone like them stepping up to lead. They'll flock to you like moths to a flame. It's already happening: Just in the first six months of 2017, even in special election losses, Democrats have shifted the margins in our direction in four Republican districts that Trump won.

But don't wait for a plan on how to talk to Trump voters to come down from some mythical unicorn of a leader. You understand better than anyone what "progressive" means in your home. You know what policies could appeal to even your most conservative neighbors, and you know how to connect them to your life. You're the progressive ambassador to your community—even if you don't get their votes, you'll make sure they aren't just hearing a singular viewpoint.

Winning isn't the only thing that matters. Just by running, you're holding your elected official accountable. And there's a pretty good chance Democrats in your area haven't had someone to vote for in a while. Go to page 27 for more on why running—win or lose—matters.

It doesn't matter if you live in a blue state, either.

I talk to first-time candidates constantly. No one ever says to me: "I live in a competitive district where at any given point, either a Republican or a Democrat could win." Whether you'd describe your community as red, blue, or something else entirely, remember: no one has it easy. Just jump in and compete.

No one ever says, "Adidas, you're the only ones allowed to make shoes," or "Gap, J.Crew makes the best jeans, you're not allowed to make jeans anymore." But in politics, limited competition is accepted because the "establishment" operates from a place of limited resources, scarcity of time, and hubris. Don't be afraid of a primary if you have something to say.

> ■ In this book, the "establishment," or "party," is defined as the network of organizations, including the Democratic National Committee (DNC), the Democratic Congressional Campaign Committee (DCCC), the Democratic Senatorial Campaign Committee (DSCC), the Democratic Legislative Campaign Committee (DLCC), the Democratic Governors Association (DGA), the state parties, and all affiliated groups. In the interest of full transparency, I have worked with these organizations in the past and likely will again throughout my career. I think they do a lot of things well! However, they are sometimes shortsighted and often burdened by so much institutional bullshit that Democrats' victories are frequently in spite of their work and not because of it.

THE WAY CANDIDATE RECRUITMENT IS "TRADITIONALLY" DONE

Typically, the establishment will target an open race or a vulnerable Republican incumbent. Then the staff and elected officials in the area will search for someone they or their networks know in the district (or they'll literally uproot someone, move them to the district, and get them on the ballot).

In the past, this has inherently limited the talent pool to a particular network, perpetuating a cycle of typically older white men and their staffs or friends running for office. It also limits the geographic reach of the party: If you're a Democrat who wants to run in an otherwise safe district, you're on your own.

The party chooses candidates who are seen as "viable," meaning they can raise money. In politics, "money" is understood to be shorthand for electability and success. If you can inspire people to financially invest in your campaign, it's assumed that you can inspire people to vote for you, too. Until people vote, money is the clearest measure of which candidate is able to get support in a meaningful way. This means the party tends to search for people with wealthy networks, since a candidate's first round of fundraising prospects will come from his or her immediate circle.

This all assumes the party recruits for that office at all. The DCCC and DSCC are focused on federal races, and most state parties aren't actively recruiting for races beyond state legislatures and perhaps mayoral races in bigger cities. No one is wholly responsible for finding the next generation of leaders to run for positions on city councils, county boards, school boards, and the like.

Recruited candidates (or party-approved candidates) get access to money, institutional knowledge, tools, coordination, and, arguably most important, the voter file.

■ **The voter file is a list of registered voters that includes their name, address, history of voting behavior, and as much information as possible. It's the Holy Bible of a campaign. Voter files (or subsets of them) make up the initial list of who candidates needs to talk to. They require a lot of money and time to keep up to date. Each time you change your address, the party needs to update your profile in the voter file. That requires tracking you down and getting the right info. A "clean and complete voter file" is every campaign manager's dream. We'll dig into how you get one on page 96.**

The party staff believes they know who deserves that help, where they should focus their limited resources, and who should ultimately win.

That's mostly bullshit. For one thing, the party's track record is iffy at best (in no small part because there's a *lot* that happens during an election that is entirely out of anyone's control). For another, every cycle, the amount of money in politics goes up and up and up. Put aside for a moment judgment on whether that's good or bad—it's proof that the pool of resources available for political engagement is growing. But ultimately, it comes down to a simple belief: Institutions shouldn't pick the winner of an election—voters should. When the party limits access to important resources that candidates need to be successful, either because they don't want to "play in the primary" or have chosen to protect the incumbent at the expense of allowing a new voice to enter the race and have a chance to succeed, the party is discouraging people from showing up at all.

Ultimately, it is to the Democratic Party's benefit to encourage primaries and foster competition. Our best leaders come from places where there are competitive primaries! Nancy Pelosi and Kamala Harris come from California, a state with rich Democratic leadership. Chuck Schumer and Hillary Clinton came from New York, and President Barack Obama came from Chicago—both places that are flooded with Democrats. When Democratic candidates have to work harder, engage with voters, and articulate their positions, the party ultimately becomes stronger.

So if you want to run against a Democratic incumbent, take a look at who represents you and decide whether you can make a compelling and positive case for what you believe and why your leadership would matter. If you can, run.

Don't let the first person in the race scare you out of it. It's not "first to file" who wins. It's whoever the voters like. And if you're true to who you are, passionate about the problems you want to solve, and willing to put in the work, voters will like you.

You don't have be that into Politics with a capital P.

In fact, it's better that you're not into "Politics." Voters hate politicians. Voters like real people—people like you.

This is an important axiom to keep in mind: Before you run, when you run, and even if you win, you're still a voter and a citizen first. Be the kind of politician you'd want to vote for.

Voters want someone who understands their problems and who has real, lived experience. Presidential candidates get briefed each day on the price of milk in whatever city they're in because those small but meaningful details of life matter. So don't worry if you don't know that much about politics yet. You can learn the system and the rules.

> *" I did not anticipate the level of animosity toward me as a first-time candidate, especially in my district, from both the establishment figures in the party and some of the other candidates. I think there's an automatic disdain for young candidates who are running for high levels of office for the first time. People think you need experience—to have been on city council or a county commissioner, or some other entry-level position in politics—before you can move up to the next level. But in Michigan, from my perspective, we need people who haven't walked the traditional pathways to power to run for office. That means teachers, firefighters, and young entrepreneurs—folks who come at life with a different perspective."*
>
> —DARRIN CAMILLERI, Michigan state legislator,
> on entering politics for the first time

You don't need a long résumé. (And it's okay if you're young.)

Repeat after me: *Donald Trump is president.* Forget everything you've ever known about politics; you're qualified to run for office.

Seriously. As of this writing, Betsy DeVos is the secretary of education, despite not believing we should have a public education system. Rick Perry is the secretary of energy despite saying in a presidential debate that he'd nix the entire agency. Ben Carson said himself that he wasn't qualified to run a federal agency and was then appointed the housing and urban development secretary.

Federal positions have age requirements (you must be twenty-five to serve in the House of Representatives, thirty to serve in the U.S. Senate, and thirty-five to be president or vice president), and some local positions may as well (usually candidates must be at least eighteen or in their mid-twenties), but there is no rule that says you need ten years of experience to be a school board member or fifteen years in the workforce to serve on city council.

What you do need, however, is experience as a member of the community. You need to intrinsically understand the people you're trying to represent. Maybe that means you've volunteered with a local nonprofit, or maybe you're a small-business owner. Maybe you're a regular at the community center bingo night and you know all the folks at the local deli. Résumés don't matter but deep roots do.

You don't have to be rich.

Don't think you have to fund your race yourself. In fact, it's better that you don't. Fundraising is hard and often exhausting, but it's how you get people invested in your race. You know who's most likely to vote for you? Someone who's given you money and is financially invested in your success. (I'll talk a lot about how to ask people for money starting on page 141. Don't worry about it for the moment.)

That being said: While you don't need to be a billionaire or a millionaire like Trump, you should be financially stable. If you're living paycheck to paycheck, running might seriously hurt your financial health. But if you've got your financial house in order, there will be ways to make it work.

You don't need to be a policy wonk.

See: Donald Trump, who needs a *Schoolhouse Rock!* refresher on how a bill becomes a law.

You can learn the ins and outs of policy on the job. You can get help from people who lovingly geek out over the tax code and who will patiently walk you through every line of a new zoning ordinance. You don't have to be an expert in everything. You do have to be passionate about what drives you and be willing to listen, learn, and accept that objective truths exist and facts matter. If you can do all that, you'll be okay.

"As women, I think we—I mean, I—feel nervous about not being an expert on everything. But you don't have to know everything. I think the merits of being a good leader are surrounding yourself with people who know more than you or are experts in different things. Being comfortable asking questions, or saying you don't have that information and getting it from people who do, is just as valuable as having the information yourself."

—LIZ DOERR, school board member in Richmond, VA,
on knowing what you don't know

You don't have to be a lawyer.

We need more teachers, scientists, technologists, social workers, nurses, doctors, stay-at-home parents, veterans, janitors, professors, students, entrepreneurs, writers, artists, and whatever-you-ares to run for office. Your experience and your perspective will make you better at governing; you'll come at this with fresh eyes and a unique viewpoint.

Lawyers are great, and if you're a lawyer who wants to run, do it. But if you're not a lawyer, don't think you're not welcome. You are.

And you definitely don't need to be perfect, online or off.

Four Reasons Why It's Okay to Be a Flawed Human

1. There's a concept in punditry and media theory called the Overton window—also known as "the window of discourse"—used to describe the range of ideas the public will accept. Simply put, an idea that is absolutely bananas is at one end of the Overton window; an idea that is accepted policy is at the other. Before Trump ran for office, if you had predicted that a presidential candidate (or any candidate) would be "a millionaire who once called the 1980s his 'personal Vietnam' because he managed to have a lot of sex without catching an STD," you would have been laughed out of the room. Trump's victory pushed the limits of what we deem to be

15

appropriate behavior for a political candidate. There's almost no chance you've tweeted something worse than what Trump has tweeted. It's unlikely there are any photos of you as ridiculous as some of the photos of him. And while the rules didn't quite apply to him, don't worry. The public has shown the outer limits of what they're willing to tolerate from a public official. You're probably fine.

2. Presidential and congressional races often get nasty and personal. School board and city council races are almost never nasty or personal. The people you're talking to every day will know the real you and not the you they see in headlines.

3. The kinds of mistakes most people make are quickly becoming normalized for our elected officials. As we begin to flood the zone with scores of people who've grown up on the internet and have lived in public for much of their lives, it stops being interesting when someone has a silly tweet or Instagram post, because everyone has one of those.

4. Think about the politicians you like and respect. Are they perfect people with scripted talking points and perfectly polished personas? No. They're the ones who get a little sassy on Twitter, or who Snapchat like a real person, or who post family recipes on the internet every holiday. Your flaws make you real and genuine—you are the kind of person many politicians have to be coached into being. Lean into it.

That being said: It's important to recognize the land mines. Be aware of your strengths, your weaknesses, your regrets, your financial difficulties, and your personal scandals. Everything known can be handled—it's the secrets that get you in the end. (As the expression goes: It's not the crime, it's the cover-up.) Anything that you might imagine is a deal-breaker probably isn't. Are you in student debt? Did you have to refinance your house? Do you have a photo of you in college playing beer pong? None of those are deal-breakers as long as you and your team know about them.

You can't wait. If you want to stop Trump, you have to run now.

Resisting Trump's agenda starts at the local level. When Trump signed an executive order promising to halt funding to municipalities that didn't cooperate with his immigration rulings, mayors fought back. They established their cities as sanctuary cities. They said no. When Trump announced his intention to pull out of the Paris Accord, devastating the global fight to prevent climate change, city and state leadership stepped up to sign on themselves.

The headlines might cover what's happening in Congress or in the courts, but in your community, resistance looks like community centers welcoming refugees in for dinner, cities finding new funding for health care centers that Trump's budget might cut, or school boards promising to protect trans kids' rights even if Trump's government won't. Local leaders—city council members, school board members, mayors, and state legislators—are leading the charge because they are in direct contact with the people who are hurt by these policies.

You don't have to win to be a leader. Just by running, you will have a platform to advocate. You'll be able to get press, organize people, galvanize support, and engage people around your values.

Too many people are restless because they're angry and brokenhearted but have no place to channel that energy. A campaign solves that problem—for you and for your community.

Running right now, win or lose, matters.

Things That Make a Real, Tangible, Long-Term Difference in People's Lives

Running for office and winning, then governing to serve your constituents

Running for office and losing, having held your elected officials accountable

Supporting candidates who will govern according to your values by volunteering, donating, and voting

Voting in every election from here on out, regardless of whether or not you feel particularly inspired—because it's your civic duty to show up

Things That Don't Make a Real, Tangible, Long-Term Difference in People's Lives

Complaining

After all, waiting to get involved is part of the reason we're in this mess in the first place.

Donald Trump can govern basically unchecked by Congress because we ("we" being progressives who give a shit about what happens to our country) didn't push ourselves in a big way to get involved on the local level.

Let's zoom out: Members of Congress are more partisan than ever. According to partisanship scores commonly used by academics, Democrats have gotten a little bit more liberal and Republicans have gotten a lot more conservative.[4]

This is in part because of everyone's favorite buzzword: *gerrymandering*.

On the congressional level, gerrymandering has created a system in which the only contest that really matters is the primary. In order to win that contest, a politician needs to appeal to primary voters, and primary voters tend to be the most dedicated, most passionate people—the extremists. (This is true regardless of party.)

That's how we got whackadoodle conservative congressmen. And that's how we got a Congress that seems unlikely to ever impeach Donald Trump (although I hope I'm wrong about that)—and in fact will stand behind even his craziest acts and proclamations. Yes, it's because they have no spine and no moral conscience. But it's also because the only constituents they need to pay attention to in order to ensure reelection are the folks who vote in their primaries, and the people who vote in Republican primaries are Trump Republicans.

Gerrymandering is the reason for all that—and gerrymandering is driven by our state legislatures, who redraw the districts after each census. (Best way to fix it: Get more progressives like you into local government and pushing for independent commissions to draw new boundaries. You are the solution.)

In 2017, Republicans ran the show in state capitals. As of this writing, Republicans control both chambers in thirty-two states, including seventeen with veto-proof majorities—those thirty-two states account for 61 percent of the U.S. population. Democrats control the legislature in just thirteen states (representing only 28 percent of the population) and have veto-proof majorities in only five.

Republicans have governor's mansions in thirty-four states, while Democrats only have sixteen (though the Alaskan governor, who ran as an independent, is supported by Democrats).

This isn't an accident. For the last decade, Republicans have had a national strategy to explicitly take over state Houses. They've moved around hundreds of millions of dollars to fund state and local races with a particular goal: Win state Houses so they can gerrymander the fuck out of Congress (and drag policy-making on the local level as far right as they can).

The Koch brothers have invested huge amounts of money in this and in talent development writ large—they've even set up an organization called the Leadership Institute, with an annual budget of more than $30 million. There is no comparable progressive organization with the same kind of money.

Democrats are a bit behind on this, for reasons that are beyond the scope of this book and are regularly debated on Twitter, if you're interested. But as a party, we're working on it. And you can be a part of the solution. Don't wait for someone to tell you it's your turn. Step up and run.

The only thing you really need to have to run is the right motivation.

Don't run because you want to *be* something. Run because you want to *do* something. Run because there's a problem you want to solve and an office that lets you solve it.

There is a type of campaigning that some folks have called "conviction politics"—that's a jargony way of saying something simple: Run on your values and ideas rather than trying to adapt to fit the consensus or take positions that are popular in the polls.

It's not complicated. If you believe in something, say it. If you disagree with something, say that, too. Take a stand, be informed, have an opinion, and base it on your values.

Saying your true opinion is honestly just so much easier than trying to figure out where the people are and then following their lead. If you're not being true to your gut, you'll end up tired on the trail one day and slipping up, doing your campaign more long-term damage by undermining your own credibility.

It feels peak cliché to say it, but it's true: Just be your best, most authentic self.

Good Reasons to Run for Office the First Time

You have a specific problem you want to solve and there's an office that lets you solve it.

Your elected official isn't representing your values.

You believe your particular community is underrepresented in your government.

Bad Reasons to Run for Office the First Time

You can win.

You want to run for a bigger office in four years.

You think the title sounds nice.

You're holding a grudge.

The perks are cool.

The power!!

Grad school is too expensive and this seems more fun.

Be willing to work hard.

This is the most important requirement. Campaigns are hard work. They'll break you down and build you back up. Your entire life might change.

People who work on campaigns professionally will tell you that doing so is the best/worst/hardest/scariest/most important thing you could do with your life. Candidates feel that even more. The pressure is unimaginable. The public scrutiny is penetrating. The hours are infinite and the work is sometimes exciting, but more often it's grinding and menial.

But to use yet another cliché, nothing good comes easy, and serving your community is genuinely doing good. It *should* be hard work to run for office. You *should* have to hustle to talk to voters, knock on doors, and earn your constituents' trust. If you win your election, you'll be making decisions that will directly impact their lives. They should be asking you tough questions, holding you accountable, and demanding to know what you believe. You're their representative. Once they give you their vote, you'll be their eyes, ears, and voice—you'll be in the room where it happens, fighting for your people.

Serving in elected office is an incredible privilege. You have to earn it. But you don't have to be a rich old white male lawyer with a flawless background to have the chance to try.

> "*I had a full-time–plus job that required fifty or sixty hours a week of my time. I was raising my sons (we have three) and I was campaigning at night and on weekends. It can be exhausting, but almost always exhilarating. I'm a high-energy person, always have been, but anyone running—and doing it right—should be prepared to commit the time and energy.*"
>
> —CHERI BUSTOS, congresswoman from Illinois, on the hardest part of her first campaign

A Pep Talk
by Emmy Ruiz

Nevada and Colorado State Director for Hillary Clinton's 2016 presidential campaign
| Political Director of Annie's List

Hey. Stop looking around and wondering what if.

No doubt about it, we are living in uncertain times. Donald J. Trump is president of the United States and working hard to turn back the clock on every civil rights victory our country has fought for. *Every single one of them.*

But our country has been through painful times before. We cannot forget that during our country's history there have been plenty of hard truths to overcome. And there will be more.

It wasn't that long ago that slavery in our country was legal. That black and brown kids were segregated in schools. That women didn't have the right to vote or make our own decisions about our bodies. Hell, today women are still not paid for equal work—and the pay gap is even worse for women of color.

Black men and women are being harmed by our country's policing and incarceration practices. Our families are being torn apart. More so than at any time before, immigrants are a political target. State legislature after state legislature has rolled back the clock on our voting rights and on protective measures for women's health.

Elections matter. Policies matter. And above all, the people who represent you and your family matter.

Every election, whether it is for the school board or the U.S. Senate, has consequences. And the sad truth is that in our country, communities of color and women will be disproportionately affected by the decisions our current elected officials (Republicans) will make. It is unconscionable.

Election Day 2016 was yet another painful reminder that there is still so much progress to be made. There are more questions than answers right now, but we've all got a choice to make. We can stand up for what's right, we can speak up for the voiceless, or we can pretend as if nothing has occurred and keep wondering what if.

Who is going to help? What can be done? How can we best resist?

Stop looking around and asking yourself these questions. There is only one person I want you to take a closer look at.

You.

Because what if it's you? Starting today, see yourself as the leader our communities and country deserve. Yes, you. Do everything you can to elect someone who represents us all: you.

Why? Because you're you. Because you care. Because of the unique story that only you can tell. Because you are a woman. Because you are a person of color. Because if not you, who else? Our country and democracy deserve *you*.

Think of the life you've lived and what has shaped you most. Maybe it's that you, like most of our country, are drowning in college debt, or that, like mine, your parents are immigrants, and you've seen how hard they've worked to live the American dream.

I'm begging you. Run for office. Run for something. Lead something. Raise your hand. Jump into the fight.

I was Hillary Clinton's state director in Nevada. It was the final days before the caucus, and we were tied with Senator Sanders and spending the day going from event to event.

During one event, a young girl named Karla raised her hand and asked Hillary Clinton about her parents. She started to cry, worried that they would be deported. Hillary held her in her arms to answer her question and promised she would do everything she could to help her.

Would a Republican today have the same reaction to our moment with Karla? This moment is an example of leadership. Leadership with heart, warmth, and purpose.

Right now, our country is made up of more than 50 percent women and almost 40 percent are people of color, but our elected officials and people in leadership do not reflect that.

Only 19 percent of the U.S. Congress is made up of women and people of color. You can do the math. It's on all of us to change that.

Okay, you convinced me. Maybe I could run for office, but how?

It's not going to be easy, but fighting for what's right is always worth it. Follow these easy steps and jump into the ring.

Define your values: What are you fighting for and who do you care about the most? What kind of leader do you want to be? What are the issues that move you in your own community? For example, think of all the young Dreamers (those who benefit from the Obama administration's Development, Relief, and Education for Alien Minors Act) in our country who go to school, scared sick they might never see their parents again. They are who I'm fighting for.

Decide what office you are running for: Where does your passion lie? If you care about education, it might make sense for you to start by running for school board or to be a university regent. If you want to take on the corruption in Washington, run for Congress! The possibilities are endless. Ultimately, you get to decide.

Invest in people power: Your family, friends, colleagues, and people are your most precious resources. They will help you raise the early money you need to get started, build your network, and get the word out about the race you are running. Until you start to build out your staff, volunteers are critical to help you do the work. Start by asking the people who love and know you the most.

Be bold: There is too much on the line for any of us to hesitate or to not speak up for what we believe. Martin Luther King Jr. once said, "In the end, we will remember not the words of our enemies, but the *silence* of our friends." Now is the time for action and for speaking up.

What I'm asking you to do is to commit to bold leadership—a type of bold leadership that always stands up for what is right, speaks up when necessary (and even when not), and always asks the question "Are we lifting each other up right now?"

Don't get me wrong. Running for office won't be easy, but doing the right thing is always worth it. And of course, you might lose.

But every single day you will have the opportunity to win. You win when you listen to someone who has never felt heard, when someone volunteers for the first time, and when you elevate the issues that truly affect people's lives. But above all, our communities win. We get to write the definition of what it means to "win."

People are starved for leadership and, like you, are looking for direction. For a second, imagine the impact you will have on a young Latina who has never seen anyone who looks like her run for office. In you, she will see herself and know that anything is possible.

If you run a campaign based on values and empowering people, running for office will be a life-changing experience. And if you're not going to do it for you, do it for those who need us most.

So stop looking around. It's you we've all been waiting for. Look at yourself and jump in. Be bold. Run for office. Help someone run for office. Change the face of power in our country.

It's not just that I'm asking you to stop looking around and start looking at yourself; it's that it is on us. It's our turn. It's our responsibility to speak up and fight for our communities.

2

WHY WINNING ISN'T EVERYTHING
(OR, AN EXCUSE TO TALK ABOUT THE UTTER BULLSHIT THAT IS THE UNCONTESTED ELECTION)

■ **One of the fundamental premises** of democracy is that voters get a choice in who represents them. A voter goes to the polls, sees their options, and picks the one they want. If a voter doesn't like the incumbent, he or she has an alternative.

We've failed to live up to that premise at every level of government. We've let uncontested elections, in which there is only one person on the ballot—usually an incumbent—become the norm.

Every day I get a Google Alert for "uncontested" (FYI, I'm learning a lot about uncontested divorces and a racehorse named Uncontested.) Just a few of the many, many examples:

- In 2017, in Macon County, Illinois, 120 of 174 races were considered no-contest.[5]

- In 2015, 78 percent of school board races in Washington State went uncontested.[6]

- In New Jersey, more than half of the 1,528 school board seats went uncontested, and 130 of the positions had literally zero candidates.[7]

- In 2016, in Wisconsin, regardless of population, only 4 percent to 5 percent of municipalities reported two or more candidates for each board seat, and in 52 percent of communities, there was one or no candidate for each seat.[8]

- In 2016, 40 percent of the 7,383 state legislative races were uncontested. Eighty-two percent of Georgia's state representative races were uncontested, making the state's legislature the least competitive in the country. Other states where 50 percent or more of the races were uncontested: Arizona, Delaware, Illinois, Louisiana, Massachusetts, New Mexico, South Carolina, and Texas.[9]

- In twenty-four of Los Angeles County's eighty-eight cities, elections were canceled at least once between 2004 and 2014.[10] In 2016, Ohio considered legislation literally formalizing this process for primaries; this would prevent folks from even writing in an alternative.[11]

- In 2016, House of Representatives candidates were uncontested in Alabama, Arkansas, Pennsylvania, Illinois, New York, Massachusetts, Georgia, and Texas. [12]

- In Vermont, in 2016, Democrat Peter Welch also appeared as the Republican nominee because enough voters wrote in his name on the primary ballot.[13]

- In Texas, in 2016, Hillary Clinton won Republican Congressman Pete Sessions's House district—but because Democrats didn't field a candidate, all those people who showed up to vote for her had no alternative but to vote for Rep. Sessions.[14]

In local primaries, it's even worse: Incumbents win reelection simply by showing up.

In the 2014 elections, only 5 percent of people lived in a state legislative district with a truly competitive primary, meaning a race where the margin of victory was 5 percent or less. But that's a deceptive stat, because usually, if Republicans have a competitive primary, Democrats don't, and vice versa. [15]

Because of gerrymandering in many of these districts, whoever wins that primary wins the general election. Consider that twenty-seven million people voted in 2014 state legislative primaries, while 107 million people voted in the 2014 state legislative general elections. Those twenty-seven million people had a whole lot more influence than the 104 million, because they were *actually* picking the winner.

The benefits of incumbency explain some of this: Incumbents tend to have at least a 90 percent reelection rate, in no small part because holding office means you have name recognition, an organization around you, and a platform to get press and actually deliver things for your constituents. It's scarier and harder to challenge an incumbent.

But some of the blame has to go to the party institutions. The parties often don't field candidates in elections where the result is somewhat fated (or seems that way based on past election results and demographics). The parties have limited resources both in terms of money and people, so they focus on getting "good" candidates in winnable districts instead of on making sure there's a person on the ballot for every office.

Sure, sometimes the institutions know who's going to win. But sometimes they don't! Or sometimes they think they do and then the unexpected happens (see: 2016). Sometimes an incumbent can get indicted, or get sick, or make a gaffe so debilitating they have no chance of winning. Sometimes they have to drop out.

The establishment might rationalize that they don't devote time and money to recruiting candidates because registration and expected turnout is low, so it doesn't matter who's on the ballot. I call bullshit: Voters don't show up in some of these places because, more often than not, there's no one to vote for. If our values aren't on the ballot, then our values don't even have a chance of winning.

Uncontested elections have severe consequences. We citizens suffer when we aren't given a choice.

A study from 2011 found that by looking at roll-call vote participation and bill introduction and enactment, state legislators elected in unopposed contests quite literally govern worse than legislators who have to run in competitive contests.[16] This makes unfortunate sense. If an elected official is going to be held accountable for their actions and be made to defend them to voters, they take those actions a little bit more seriously. A politician who's going to have to actually campaign on their record instead of just doing a cakewalk to the polls will govern with their constituents in mind.

The lack of competitive campaigns often means less voter contact. Candidates who actually have to campaign get money flowing in and organizations springing up in order to engage with people about policies and the impact government has on people. The electorate gets more informed and active, and the government better reflects what constituents want.

If people are going to get excited about local elections—and get into the habit of voting every single time—they should have someone who shares their values on the ballot to cast a vote for, every single time.

Run. You could be the first Democrat in a while to step up in a red state. Or you could be the first Democrat to challenge your incumbent in a while. Either way: You're fulfilling the basic premise of democracy. Extra brownie points for you.

When you run, try to win. But results aren't the only impact a campaign can have.

Here are the good things that happen during a campaign besides you or your preferred candidate winning:

Elected leaders are held accountable.

In an ideal world, all public officials are truly public servants—they run for office because they want to solve a problem or help their communities. (That should be you! You should run.)

In reality, some elected officials are more opportunistic than others. Some are in it for the wrong reasons. Some are picked to run and given every resource needed to win, and then the benefits of incumbency carry them along their career.

The only time they'll ever really feel pressure is when their job is on the line. If you're running against an incumbent, you'll be the one forcing that elected official to answer for what they've done and the promises they've kept or broken. You'll make them engage with their constituents and really hear what their voters want out of them. You might be the only one forcing the incumbent to talk about an issue they really don't want to discuss. Just by being on the ballot and demanding answers to questions, you'll help your community get more clarity out of your representatives.

Much of the activism that happens between elections is meant to put political pressure on an elected official and make them aware their voters are watching. It's all buildup to the breaking point when voters can actually kick someone out.

You'll increase volunteer engagement and voter contact.

Part of campaigning is building a team of volunteers who share your values and want you to succeed. You'll have friends helping you, sure, but you'll also have strangers you meet when you knock on doors, ones who you inspire to step up and help, too. You'll be helping to build a network of volunteers who want to get progressives elected.

If you're running a race the right way, those volunteers will be spending all their time talking to voters about you and about the issues. This has a benefit for the campaign, of course, but think about the benefit for voters: They're hearing from passionate people about what their government does for them, getting a chance to ask questions, and actually engaging with the issues on a human level. There is no downside to more citizen engagement.

(As a side note, for those invested in the future of the Democratic Party . . . Volunteer engagement + voter contact = party building.)

You'll become a better you.

By running, you're going to become a leader in your community. You're going to build a network of people who care about what happens next. You're going to get savvier, wiser, and more comfortable talking to strangers and doing public speaking, and you're going to learn the ropes of our political system.

Regardless of the results, you'll be seen as someone who can energize people and actually do something instead of just complaining about it.

Real talk . . . So you lose. Who cares?

Let's talk about some losers:

- Abraham Lincoln lost six campaigns before he won the presidency.

- Bernie Sanders ran for U.S. Senate in 1972 and got 1,571 votes—one vote for every twenty-nine votes the winner got. He lost three more statewide races for Senate and for governor of Vermont without ever getting more than 6.1 percent of the vote. (Then he ran for mayor of Burlington and won—a perfect illustration of why you should start local.)

- Bill Clinton lost his first election to an incumbent Republican member of the House of Representatives.

- Barack Obama lost an Illinois Democratic primary against Representative Bobby Rush in 2000.

- Hillary Clinton lost the Democratic primary in 2008 before she won it (and then the popular vote) in 2016.

Many people lose their first race. Losing breeds introspection. You run once, you figure out what you did right and wrong, you retool, and then you try again. On the second time (or third time) out, you do better.

Do you remember who lost the city council race in your hometown two years ago? Or who ran for school board in the last six months? This is one of the upsides of running in smaller elections. You'll get credit for trying, you'll learn new things, you'll expand your skills and build your network, and no one will give a single shit if you lose. Your community will be stronger simply because you ran.

Theodore Roosevelt, our twenty-sixth president and namesake of your favorite stuffed animal, said it well in 1910 at a speech in Paris:

> It is not the critic who counts; not the man who points out how the strong man stumbles, or where the doer of deeds could have done them better. *The credit belongs to the man who is actually in the arena,* whose face is marred by dust and sweat and blood; who strives valiantly; who errs, who comes short again and again, because there is no effort without error and shortcoming; but who does actually strive to do the deeds; who knows great enthusiasms, the great devotions; who spends himself in a worthy cause; who at the best knows in the end the triumph of high achievement, and who at the worst, if he fails, at least fails while daring greatly, so that his place shall never be with those cold and timid souls who neither know victory nor defeat.

3

CIVICS 101: HOW GOVERNMENT (GENERALLY) WORKS AT THE FEDERAL AND STATE LEVELS (OR, WHY YOU SHOULD RUN FOR LOCAL OFFICE)

■ **If you want to run for office,** you don't have to start with Congress. In fact, you shouldn't start with Congress. Local races are affordable, winnable, and manageable, especially if you're willing to knock on every door and talk to every voter.

More important: Local office matters more than federal office. Local office makes a greater impact on day-to-day life than nearly anything Congress ever does.

Not sure what I mean by "local office" versus "federal office," what "Congress" refers to, or simply need a civics refresher? I've got you covered. (There's no shame in forgetting your high school government classes.)

I'm going to dig in on the Democratic side of things since that's what I know best. If you're a Republican, the party structure is analogous and the names are relatively similar.

THE DEMOCRATIC NATIONAL COMMITTEE (DNC)

When people reference "the party" or "national Democrats," they tend to mean the DNC. Located in what is, frankly, a depressing building right near the Capitol, the DNC is run by a chair and board elected by DNC members, who in turn were elected by state party members.

The DNC's official mission is to coordinate strategy and support Democrats at every level of government, with a focus on presidential elections. They plan and execute the national conventions every four years, articulate the party's official platform, and fundraise in order to direct human and financial resources toward candidates as they deem strategically necessary.

The DNC doesn't make the rules for party or voter registration in any given state, nor does it actually run the state-by-state primary process. The DNC also doesn't have direct authority over any elected officials. The chair, leaders, and staff can try to guide messaging—and can use money as a carrot and/or stick to praise or punish elected officials—but at the end of the day, elected officials are accountable to voters, not to the committee.

There are separate committees that support candidates and Democrats in each branch of government. I'll get into those later.

STATE PARTIES

Every state has its own independent chapter of the Democratic Party, referred to as the "state party," with its own leadership structure and staff. The parties then break down even further—first by county, then town or city, and then often by precinct (also called a voting district). A precinct is made up of, on average, around one thousand people—it might be a neighborhood, or a subset of a neighborhood.

Local parties (also sometimes known as party committees) support local candidates. Theoretically, these local organizations provide the umbrella for Democrats in your area to coordinate, work together, and use resources strategically and effectively. Local party leaders at a precinct and county level decide who leads the state party, and the state party leaders then decide who leads the national party.

The state parties and local committees don't tend to have a lot of (or any) money, nor do they have nearly enough resources to do what they need to do.

But hear me out: You should join your local party.

It's very easy to dismiss the entire Democratic Party as a garbage fire—"just burn the building down" is a common refrain among some political operatives. But complaining doesn't solve the problem. Joining the party does.

If you can even find info about a local Democratic Party meeting, you're going to show up and likely see a lot of old(er) people. You'll sit through meetings with scattered agendas, grumpy curmudgeons, and conversations that seem to go around in circles without real takeaways. When you go to volunteer, you're going to get tasked with stuffing envelopes, dropping off literature, or staffing a booth at the local farmer's market.

It might not be very fun. You might get frustrated and want to wash your hands of the whole thing.

Keep coming back. Somewhere hidden in the chaos are a few good people who, like you, genuinely want to make a difference. You can find them! Volunteer to fix the website for your local committee, or run the social media accounts, or redesign the logos. Ask if you can help plan a happy hour and invite your friends; ask them if they'll each chip in $20 to the local party. When it comes time to run for local leadership, throw your name in the hat. Commit to volunteering for local candidates and become a precinct captain who organizes your friends and network to do the same.

You don't have to run for office to lead (although that's one way to do it). You can simply lead by doing; if you want to fix the Democratic Party, your best bet is to join it first.

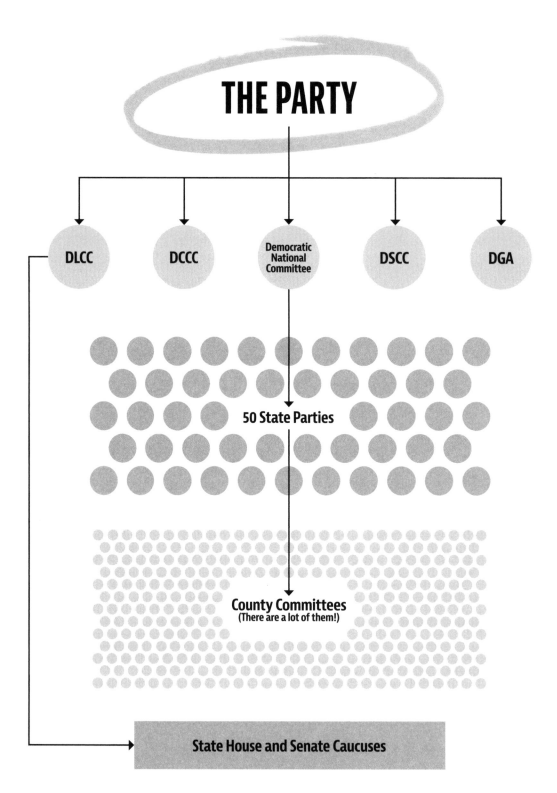

THE PARTY

DLCC DCCC Democratic National Committee DSCC DGA

50 State Parties

County Committees
(There are a lot of them!)

State House and Senate Caucuses

POLITICAL INSTITUTIONS

Outside of the parties, there are organizations like unions, interest groups, and grassroots activists that do consistent electoral work. I'll walk through those beginning on page 76.

The party structure exists to support and fill out the government at every level. So let's get into it.

A QUICK AND DIRTY GUIDE TO THE THREE BRANCHES OF THE FEDERAL GOVERNMENT

The Executive Branch

Aka the White House, or the Administration.

Who's in It The president, vice president, the president's cabinet, and everyone who works for him (or, sigh, her).

Requirements The president must be at least thirty-five years old and a natural-born citizen of the United States.

■ Caucuses are a way of holding an election in which, during a single period of time, a bunch of people gather and literally vote with their feet. People who pick candidate A will stand on one side of the room, people who pick candidate B will stand on the other side, and candidate C supporters might stand in the middle. A proportional number of delegates are then assigned out, and if any one candidate doesn't hit a "viability" threshold by earning a certain amount of support, those supporters must realign to a different side. (Permit me three sentences to editorialize: Caucuses are not democratic—your vote isn't secret and you get to change your mind. They privilege older, usually white, affluent voters who can afford to take a few hours off work or away from family responsibilities to go to a firehouse in the middle of winter and stand in a corner as a way of demonstrating who they think should be president. Caucuses should be abolished.)

How We Elect the Executive Branch The president and vice president are technically elected by the electoral college after (not nearly enough) people vote on the first Tuesday after the first Monday in November every four years. Leading up to that Election Day, the country goes through two hellish years of a fucked-up nightmare of party primaries and caucuses, conventions, foreign intervention, sexism, and racism. (Hopefully that's true just the one time.)

What the Executive Branch Does The president is supposed to sign laws after Congress has passed them. The president also nominates thousands of people to fill positions in the cabinet, agencies, and the federal courts. Critically, the president is commander-in-chief of the armed forces. The vice president has no real duties but is the technical president of the Senate and is in charge of breaking ties.

How Old They Are Old.

How White They Are Very. All but the one.

How Male They Are One hundred percent.

How Much They Get Paid The president makes $400,000 a year while in office, along with an allowance for additional expenses. The vice president makes $230,700 a year, along with a limited expense account.

Fun fact: Retired presidents get a pension—it is equal to whatever current members of the cabinet make.

How Much It Costs to Run Too fucking much.

The Legislative Branch

Aka Congress. Every two years we get a new Congress, and each one is numbered. The 115th Congress was sworn in on January, 2017, after the 2016 election.

Who's in It Congress is made up of two chambers: the House of Representatives and the U.S. Senate. The House has 435 members, allocated based on population. The Senate has a hundred members, two per state.

Requirements To be in the House, you must be at least twenty-five years old, a citizen of the United States for seven years, and at the time of election a resident of your district.

To be in the Senate, you must be thirty years old, a citizen of the U.S. for at least nine years, and at the time of the election a resident of your state.

How We Elect the Members of the Legislative Branch All 435 members of the House are on the ballot every two years. The Senate has six-year terms and does elections in waves—one-third of the chamber is on the ballot every two years.

What the Legislative Branch Does Congress is supposed to write and pass laws, provide oversight of the executive branch, and advise and consent on nominations put forward by the executive. I use the phrase "supposed to" because these days, well, members of Congress seem to go on TV a lot. One day, you should run for Congress and change that.

Fun fact: The number of electoral votes a state gets is determined based on congressional delegation—the number of people representing a state in the House plus one for each senator.

How Old They Are The average age in the House is fifty-eight; the average age in the Senate is sixty-two.

How White They Are Very! Eighty percent of the 115th Congress identify as white.

How Male They Are Very! (Are you sensing a trend?) Only 19 percent of the 115th Congress are women.

How Much They Get Paid Most members of Congress make $174,000 per year—people in leadership positions make a bit more. Retired congressmen and women receive a pension.

How Much It Costs to Run Campaigns for House seats can cost anywhere from $500,000 to $2 million. Senate seats tend to cost anywhere from $1 million to $25 million. That number varies dramatically from state to state and depends on the competitiveness of the election and the cost of the media market.

For example, the most expensive Senate race in 2016 was in Florida, where Marco Rubio spent $50 million to protect his seat. The most expensive House race in 2016 was in Arizona, where a Republican incumbent spent $6.7 million to protect her seat. (It's worth noting: professional slimeball Paul Ryan actually raised and spent the most money, $13 million, but much of that went to other Republicans running for Congress.) That money doesn't include any groups who might have spent additional funds to run ads or put volunteers on the ground in these races.

Generally speaking, the "experts" recommend that you shouldn't run for a seat in the House unless you can pretty quickly figure out how you'll raise at least $300,000 from your network. For senators, that number is much, much bigger.

Organizations to Know The Democratic Congressional Campaign Committee (DCCC, or the "D-Trip") and the National Republican Congressional Committee (NRCC) support House candidates. The Democratic Senatorial Campaign Committee (DSCC) and the National Republican Senatorial Committee (NRSC) support Senate candidates.

■ "Tables," in politics, refers to groups of organizations or donors who coordinate strategy or, more often, money.

All of these groups are headquartered out of DC and are chaired by elected officials and staffed by political operatives. They all serve a similar purpose: that of funneling money and institutional resources to chosen candidates and helping to protect incumbents. They hire staff, run coordinated campaigns, sometimes participate in tables, and run ads on behalf of candidates. Like the DNC, these committees don't set policy positions—those are driven by the elected officials themselves.

Some of this campaign work is done out of the committee directly, and other pieces of it are directed out of the "independent expenditure" arm of the organization that legally doesn't communicate directly with the candidates.

(If you're confused, that's okay. It's a clusterfuck.)

The Judicial Branch

Aka the judiciary.

Who's in It The Supreme Court and a web of federal courts across the country.

Requirements You go to law school, work as a lawyer for a while, probably clerk for a few judges, build a network, and get a reputation in the community. You relationship-manage your way up the ladder to get appointed to bigger and more influential judgeships.

How We Elect Members of the Judicial Branch We don't. The president nominates people, and our representatives in Congress approve (or don't) of those nominations. Judges in the Supreme Court, the court of appeals, and the district courts are appointed for life until they resign, retire, die, or are impeached.

What They Do They help interpret laws and regulate arguments between other branches of government. Judges are likely our saving grace during the Trump era.

How Old They Are Old.

How White They Are Very.

How Male They Are Very. Only 4 of the 112 people to ever serve on the Supreme Court have been women—and three of them served at the same time. (May the Lord protect Ruth Bader Ginsburg, forever and ever, amen.) Across the rest of the federal judiciary, about one-third of judges are women.

How Much They Make Judges' salaries vary depending on the court—they hover in the $180,000 to $220,000 range.

How Much It Costs to Run Not applicable, since you don't run to become a judge.

LEARN MORE ON THE INTERNET Your first stop is www.uscourts.gov.

HOW THEY ALL WORK TOGETHER

These branches interact as a system of "checks and balances"—for example, Congress can pass a bill, the president can veto it (or refuse to sign it), and, with enough votes, Congress can override that veto. Or the president can issue an executive order; then the judiciary can rule it as overreaching or unconstitutional and deem it moot.

The Federal Election Commission (FEC) oversees all federal elections and deals with campaign finance rules, election laws, and administration.

■ Recommendation: Watch *Schoolhouse Rock!*'s "I'm Just a Bill." Seriously. It's catchy as hell and, more importantly, it lays out the process involved in making a bill into a law, even if that process doesn't really work anymore because of filibustering, reconciliation, and the utter bullshit of our congressional processes.

FOR MORE DETAILS . . .

People write books, teach classes, and devote their lives to explaining and understanding how our federal government works—or, more often, how it doesn't work. Read the newspaper in print. You'll be surprised at what you discover as you flip through the pages—the stories you wouldn't seek out or won't see on Twitter are the ones you need to read the most.

State government is a whole different ball game.

The Tenth Amendment of the U.S. Constitution explicitly states: "The powers not delegated to the United States by the Constitution, nor prohibited by it to the States, are reserved to the States respectively, or to the people."

What that means in practice: The federal government can't do anything not explicitly written in the Constitution. The states, accordingly, have a lot of power.

Because there is no national standard regarding how a state must structure its government, every state has its own constitution and its own way of doing things. And because elections are administered at the local level, there are different rules about spending, fundraising, and reporting—so it's a little harder to pin down specific numbers in any all-encompassing way. The numbers I toss out here are general; if you decide to run for one of these offices, get ready to go down a Google wormhole.

> ■ Generally speaking, at the statewide level, every state has the same three branches as the federal government: an executive, a judiciary, and a legislature.

The State Executive Branch

Every state is run by an elected governor; most states have a few other elected members of the executive branch, like the lieutenant governor (or vice governor), attorney general, secretary of state, comptroller (or auditor), treasurer, commissioner, and more. The roles and responsibilities of each position vary by state.

How We Elect Its Members Governors tend to serve four-year terms (except in New Hampshire and Vermont, where terms are two years long) and are elected on the first Tuesday following the first Monday in November during even-numbered years, with a few exceptions (Virginia and New Jersey, notably). Term limits vary from state to state.

What They Do Governors tend to be very practically powerful. They usually have control over government budgets and the appointing of government positions, and have a role in legislation. They might also be the commander-in-chief of the state's National Guard and the state's defense force. They often have the power to pardon a criminal sentence or restore voting rights.

How Old They Are In thirty-five states, you have to be thirty years old to run for governor. In some states, that requirement is as low as twenty-five, twenty-one, or even eighteen. Oddly enough, in Oklahoma, you have to be thirty-one.

How Male They Are Very. At the time of writing, only thirty-six women total have ever served as governor or acting governor. That's bullshit.

How White They Are Very. In 2017, forty-seven out of fifty governors are white. That's also bullshit.

How Much They Get Paid Annual salaries for governors range from $70,000 to $190,923. Governors are not usually the highest-paid state employee; those tend to be the basketball or football coach at the major state university. (As the old saying goes: Show me your budget and I'll show you your values.)

> *" In North Carolina, we technically have a part-time legislature. Therefore, maintaining a day job is necessary both before and after serving. Balancing being a full-time employee with the constant grind of a campaign becomes critical. You quickly need to learn how to carefully structure and maximize your schedule."*
>
> —CHAZ BEASLEY, North Carolina state legislator, on balancing governing and a full-time job

How Much It Costs to Run Millions—often tens of millions. In some states, upward of $150 million can be spent on a gubernatorial race. It's not cheap.

Organizations to Know The National Governors Association (NGA), the Democratic Governors Association (DGA), and the Republican Governors Association (RGA). The NGA is bipartisan and doesn't get involved in elections. The

DGA and the RGA are explicitly partisan and act as the "institutions" supporting gubernatorial races. They help campaigns hire staff, run ads, and do polling, and they direct money and resources to the campaigns.

LEARN MORE ON THE INTERNET Go to [YOUR STATE].gov. (For example: ohio.gov, texas.gov, california.gov.)

The State Judicial Branch

Most states have a supreme court (or court of appeals) that is the "court of last resort" for the state judicial system. Both the structure of these systems as well as the method of picking judges for these courts varies from state to state. Since the state variations are bananas, I'll skip an in-depth look here and let you Google (or Bing, or Ask Jeeves or Siri, or whatever) if you want to learn more. You're welcome.

LEARN MORE ON THE INTERNET Google "[YOUR STATE]" + "judiciary." The National Center for State Courts also has a handy index for all states at www.ncsc.org.

The State Legislative Branch

If you're thinking about running for office for the first time, this is where it gets relevant: You can run for state legislature even if you've never run for office before. Since this branch is one you should consider, it deserves its own chapter.

4

WHY YOU CAN ACTUALLY RUN FOR STATE LEGISLATURE

A REVIEW OF THE STRUCTURES

Forty-nine states have what's called a bicameral legislature—just like the federal government, it has two chambers. (Nebraska, that special snowflake, just has one chamber, commonly called the "Senate.") A quick breakdown of how they differ . . .

The Upper Chamber

Aka the Senate.

Who State Senators Represent Thanks to the Supreme Court decision in *Reynolds v. Sims* in 1964, all state Senate districts must be drawn to equally represent the same number of people. In California, that means a state senator represents nearly one million people. In North Dakota, a state senator represents 14,310 people. On average, each of the 1,971 state senators represents 156,399 Americans.

Some state senates only have twenty members, while others have seventy.

How Long They Serve In thirty-one states, senators serve a four-year term. In twelve states, senators serve a two-year term. In seven states, terms vary depending on the proximity of the election to the reapportionments that happen after the federal census is collected every ten years. (Those states have what's known as 2-4-4 terms, since senators will serve one two-year term and two four-year terms.) You can see why this gets complicated quickly.

In the twelve states with two-year terms, all state Senate seats are on the ballot every two years. Twenty-seven states have staggered elections, where half of the state Senate seats are up for reelection during the general elections every two years. In the eleven other states, all seats come up during the same year, so there are often general-election years where there are no state Senate seats on the ballot.

> LEARN MORE ON THE INTERNET Google "[YOUR STATE] state Senate." Look for a website with ".gov" in the URL for official information. You might find ballotpedia.org to be an invaluable resource.

The Lower Chamber

In most states it's known as the House of Representatives, though some states call their lower chamber the House of Delegates or General Assembly.

Who State Legislators Represent State House districts track with population growth. California's assembly members represent 465,674 Americans each, while New Hampshire state representatives serve 3,291 people each. On average, state representatives serve 59,626 Americans each.

How Many There Are In 2017, there are 5,413 state representatives across the country. Some states have forty-person chambers; others have more than four hundred members.

How Long They Serve Either two or four year terms.

LEARN MORE ON THE INTERNET Google "[YOUR STATE] legislature." Look for a website with ".gov" in the URL for official information.

Some Facts on Both

Commonly, both chambers are treated as parts of a singular body known as the "state legislature."

At the local level, the state legislative elections are generally spearheaded by a combination of the state parties and state House or Senate caucuses. This is where the terminology gets a little messy, so stay with me.

In each chamber, the elected officials in the party make up the caucus, or organization, which has its own staff and strategy. Elected officials raise money for both themselves and the caucus, and then the caucus reallocates funds as the leadership deems effective. The caucuses are typically responsible for recruiting candidates to fill open seats and will be wary of people challenging incumbents.

Ignore that wariness; if you want to challenge an incumbent and can make a positive argument as to why, do it.

Organizations to Know The Democratic Legislative Campaign Committee (DLCC) and the Republican Legislative Campaign Committee (RLCC) oversee national strategy and priorities around state legislative elections.

I got 99 state legislatures (and a bitch ain't one, or something).

So you know what you're walking into, a few stats about the demographic make-up of state legislatures as of 2017:

25 % women (compared with 50 % of the U.S. population)

9 % African American (compared with 13 % of the U.S. population)

5 % Latino (compared with 17 % of the U.S. population)

Unsurprisingly, at the time of writing, women make up 34 % of Democratic lawmakers and only 17 % of Republicans. People of color make up 33 % of Democrats and a paltry 5 % of Republicans.

Forty percent of state legislators have graduate degrees or professional degrees, compared with only 11 % of the U.S. population.

The average age of all state legislators is 56, compared with 47 for the U.S. population. Women tend to be 2 years older than their male counterparts; senators tend to be 2 years older than House members.

Don't expect to get rich quick.

Some state legislatures are full-time jobs and pay accordingly. In California, legislators make more than $100,000 a year, in addition to per diem costs. New Hampshire legislators make $200 per two-year term, not including a per diem. In most states, the position is paid like a part-time job.

The salaries we pay to our state legislators are too damn low. Many people who want to serve can't afford to, and the structures of our institutions limit the type of people who can enter them. This is a huge systemic problem. The only way to fix it: Run, win, then try to pass a law that increases pay for legislators.

The costs of elections for these seats vary dramatically.

Take a look at the average costs of state legislative races in 2014, broken down by chamber.

State	Senate	House
Illinois	$588,233	$252,064
California	$521,986	$387,149
Pennsylvania	$473,140	$90,624
Texas	$415,247	$188,419
New York	$317,791	$74,281
Oregon	$289,432	$126,803
Nevada	$214,140	$64,882
Florida	$208,578	$113,629
North Carolina	$173,576	$87,008
Wisconsin	$111,90	$33,097
Iowa	$96,793	$69,749
Wyoming	$7,522	$7,392

The cost of a race tends to be determined by the size of the media market, the competitiveness, and the number of people you need to reach. Also, remember: One really expensive race can throw everything else out of whack. (Illinois's average is particularly high because of a few competitive races in the Chicago suburbs. California's is high because advertising in Los Angeles is extremely pricey.)

WHY YOU SHOULD RUN FOR STATE LEGISLATURE

State legislators have power and, unlike members of Congress, tend to actually use it—the decisions state legislators make affect the daily lives of Americans in dramatic ways.

State legislatures *matter*. Nearly every week, a state legislature does something under the radar that will piss you off—remember the infamous "bathroom bill" that discriminated against trans people in North Carolina, or the countless anti-choice legislation across the country? The best way you can stop it is by fixing it yourself. Run for state legislature, hold your representatives accountable, and demand something new.

States are considered the country's laboratories for democracy, and in this metaphor, state legislatures are the beakers and vials where the experiments bubble over. Health care is a great example: The Massachusetts legislature passed "Romneycare" in 2006 based on the premise that all citizens of Massachusetts had a right to affordable insurance. Some parts of Romneycare worked, other parts didn't—but, ultimately, 97 percent of Massachusetts residents had health coverage because of the law. Even President Obama acknowledged that Romneycare was part of the model for how he wanted to structure Obamacare. The Obama administration knew it would work because the experiment had worked in Massachusetts.

Finally, state legislatures have an impact on Congress. State legislatures redraw congressional districts every ten years and determine the blocks of voters that then determine who represents you in federal government.

■ Here's a not-even-close-to-exhaustive list of issues a state legislator might work on over the course of a year: abortion, adult education, agricultural trade, alternative fuels, antiterrorism, banking, budgets, business development, carbon policy, casino gambling, charter schools, child welfare, clean drinking water, climate change, coal mining, college affordability, consumer protection, criminal justice and mass incarceration, custody issues, disability accessibility, domestic violence, driver's licenses, economic development, education, election administration, end-of-life care, energy, farming and livestock, financial literacy, food stamps, foreclosures, fossil fuels, gun violence prevention, health care, hydraulic fracturing, immigration, internet fraud, license plates, lotteries, marijuana, Medicaid, minimum wage, mortgages, motorcycle safety, nuclear energy, non-discrimination laws, payday lending, public records, railway transit, renewable energy, recycling, same-sex marriage, school bus safety, school calendars, sentencing reform, social security, taxes, transportation funding, tobacco, tort reform, traffic safety, veterans' health, women's safety, workers' rights, and voting rights.

Local government is where shit gets real.

A necessary caveat: There are a lot of variations in how local governments work. The only rule is that there is no single set of rules. Everything from partisanship to structure to pay to requirements to responsibilities to jurisdictions to titles changes from locality to locality.

To get a sense of the options, pick a jurisdiction from the first column in the chart below and a possible position from the second column—any of these could exist in your area, depending on your state constitution and local charters.

Jurisdictions	Positions
County	Councilmember
City	Supervisor
City-county (a real thing that means something is both a "city" and a "county")	Mayor
	Alderman
Town or township	Sheriff
Village	Treasurer
Borough	Attorney
District	Commissioner
Parish (a term used only in Louisiana)	Trustee
	Comptroller
Neighborhood	Manager
Ward	Director

Many localities have some kind of representative legislature, like a board, council, or commission, and an executive—maybe it's a mayor who is elected and works separately from the city council, or maybe it's a chair of the board.

There's also a whole world of what's called "special purpose" governments designated to serve a particular function. What this means in practice: conservation districts, homeowners' associations, library boards, parks and recreation authorities, airport authorities, highway and mass transit authorities, and school districts.

Some special-purpose governments are appointed and others are elected. Go down the internet wormhole on your town and figure out what your options are.

> "As the House Minority Leader in a Republican-controlled legislature, I lose often. The key is to view these losses as an opportunity to learn, and to lose as well as possible. I will always vote in favor of legislation that moves the needle toward progress, and against legislation that harms Georgians. Those votes sometimes make a difference and yield positive outcomes. But some of the most important work you can do in the minority is to slice harmful Republican legislation into the smallest pieces possible to mitigate harm that you cannot stop outright."
>
> —STACEY ABRAMS, House Minority Leader in Georgia, on why legislative votes matter

■ For territories and Native American reservations, throw everything you know out the window. And of course, DC is different too. Our capital city is under the direct authority of Congress. The city council in DC writes laws, the mayor signs laws, and then Congress has the power to overturn those laws. DC has no actual representation in Congress beyond a nonvoting delegate.

You should consider running for city council.

Generally speaking, city councils make the rules that directly affect your day-to-day life. That pothole in front of your house? The city council can fix it. The zoning laws in your neighborhood? Yep, city council. Whether that local bar gets a 2 a.m. liquor license or a 4 a.m. liquor license? City council!

City councils deal with street maintenance, city taxes, parking meters, and public services like libraries, pools, and transportation. They often oversee utility companies in the area, so they might have a say in electricity delivery or water companies. City councils tend to be the organizations that regulate trash pickup and land use. If you want to start an open-air fresh-food market or put on a parade, your city council likely has to approve. City councils decide whether your city has to take out a loan to pay for something—and whether they'll raise your local taxes to pay back that loan.

Someone has to make those kinds of decisions. If you love where you live (or if you hate where you live and want to fix it), you need to run for city council.

To figure out what's going on in your area, here's the first step you should take.

LEARN MORE ON THE INTERNET Google "[YOUR TOWN] clerk."

Clerks are usually the keepers of the rules and guidelines for local government. You should find their website, find a working phone number, then call them. (Yes, pick up the phone and call them.) If they can't help you, they'll know who can.

When they pick up, here's what to say: "I care about [insert issue here]. What part of our local government can help me solve that?"

You could also consider running for school board.

School boards (sometimes called boards of education, school committees, school directors, or trustees) are the champions for public education and the ones putting students first.

If you're on a school board, you're responsible for employing the school superintendent; developing school district policies, curricula, and budgets; overseeing facility issues; and adopting collective bargaining agreements.

On a more existential level, school board members are responsible for the community. After all, people tend to use the quality of schools as a shortcut for assessing how "good" a town or district is—and the quality of schools is determined, in part, by the school board. (This kind of rationale is admittedly simplistic and reductive. Bear with me.)

School districts are often the largest employers in a community, and the big-picture budgetary decisions are determined by school board members.

I fucking love school boards, in part because they're way more representative than any other part of government. As of this writing, 44 percent of school board members are women. According to the National School Boards Association, in large districts, 21.8 percent of school board members are African American and 6 percent are Latino.

School board members are usually unpaid in smaller districts; in larger districts, they might receive a modest salary. If you're a school board member, you're not doing it for the glamour or the money. You're doing it because you care about the kids. Teach the kids well and everything else gets better.

LEARN MORE ON THE INTERNET Google "[YOUR STATE] school board association."

WHAT YOU DON'T NEED IN ORDER TO RUN FOR LOCAL OFFICE

Experience

Elected officials have to get their start somewhere. Local office is that "somewhere." This kind of office is the first entry point for most people getting into public service. You're not usually going up against folks with ten-page résumés or long lists of previous elected experience. You're going up against other people just like you—people who care about solving a problem.

Money

In most medium-size localities, $5,000 to $10,000 will cover all your campaign expenses. Depending on the size of your town and the office you're running for, $1,000 could cut it.

School board races are some of the most affordable elections around. Seventy-five percent of school board races cost $1,000 or less! You can do this.

The bigger the school district, the more expensive it is. In Los Angeles, for example, the 2015 race for four of the district's seven seats cost more than $1.1 million. But! Nearly half of that was for one of the four seats. The other three split the remainder. And that's Los Angeles, where the student enrollment alone would be as big as the country's twentieth-largest city.

But remember, you're not self-funding—these are not out-of-pocket figures. You're raising money from people who share in your vision of what your community could be.

> "*I think local government is everything. The fact that I can cast a vote on Wednesday night and it has an impact on Thursday morning is amazing to me. The decisions we make are not in the abstract. They have very real consequences for people, and those consequences are in your face. Local government puts issues and solutions in your face better than most, because if you don't do what you're supposed to do, you're going to hear about it at church or synagogue, on date night, at the grocery store, and at your neighbor's house.*"
>
> —ANDREW GILLUM, mayor of Tallahassee, on the importance of local government

A Thick Skin

If you're getting into public service and the spotlight, you should be okay with criticism. But local races tend to be nicer and more positive than the congressional or statewide races you're used to seeing covered on TV and in the papers. You're not getting nasty when you're running against your neighbors.

The only real requirement is time and hustle. Local elections are won and lost through voter contact. You're

■ A thing to know about local office: Elected officials tend to work in the public eye. School board meetings and city council meetings are often televised on local public access TV; work can't often happen outside of those public meetings. Even if the viewership is small, the people who tune in tend to be seriously paying attention. You have to be ready for that.

going to need to talk to voters one-on-one and introduce yourself, explain why you're running, and what you're going to do for them if you get elected. It'll take time, effort, and energy. It'll be exhausting and exhilarating. It's how you'll win.

HOW TO PICK WHICH OFFICE TO RUN FOR

Don't ask yourself which office is right for you or what you can win. Don't even ask yourself what you can afford.

Instead, ask yourself these questions: What problem do I want to solve? What do I care about? What do I read about on Twitter or Facebook that makes my blood boil? What works well that I could make work even better? Pick the problem you want to solve and understand why you want to solve it. Pick the office that lets you solve it on the most local level.

For example:

I care about voting rights because my community has been discriminated against.

State legislature lets you decide what (if any) identification voters need to bring to the polls.

I care about affordable housing because of my family's struggles to pay rent.

City council determines the zoning for housing development in your town.

I care about mental health because my best friend suffers from depression.

The county board of supervisors oversees funding for mental health centers in your area.

I care about funding for the arts because I'm an artist myself.

School boards decide whether or not arts education gets prioritized in school budgets.

I care about climate change because I believe our planet is being destroyed.

The village council determines how much tax credit someone could get for switching to solar energy.

I know this seems too simple. But it should be simple. Your entire campaign is going to be driven by this passion for solving a specific problem. You're going to spend every day thinking about it, talking about it, and advocating for it. You need to be driven by this motivation and you need to care deeply. Running for office needs to be about what you believe you can do to fix your community.

If you start by deciding on the problem you want to solve and figuring out which office lets you solve it, the decisions you make regarding your campaign message and tactics will be easier. Your North Star will push you to run a values-driven, solutions-oriented campaign with a laser-like focus on what you'll do for constituents. That's the kind of campaign voters like and respect, and, win or lose, that's the kind of campaign that moves the ball forward on the issues.

Running as a Progressive in a Red State

by Jason Kander

Founder of Let America Vote | Missouri secretary of state, 2013–17
| Member of the Missouri House of Representatives, 2009–13

■ **Some of you reading this know me,** but most of you don't. If you do know me, I have a feeling it's because I'm that Democrat who knows how to put together a rifle blindfolded.

When I announced I was going to run for Senate in Missouri in 2016, no one gave me much of a chance. People said I was crazy for running against Republican incumbent Roy Blunt, who was well-established. Pundits wanted to know why I was throwing away my career as secretary of state of Missouri. They asked why I would take such a risk. Well, I'd been through much harder than politics and campaigns. I had joined the army after September 11 and volunteered for a tour in Afghanistan. I was willing to put my life on the line for this country. I laughed at the idea that taking a political risk is hard. It's not.

Now, I ended up losing that election. A lot of us lost in 2016; Democrats got thumped across the country. There are millions and millions of people disappointed in the election results. But we have a future. The election of Donald Trump is just going to be a speed bump on our country's journey toward liberty and justice. It's going to wake us up.

You can see it across the country. Whether it's the Women's March, protests against awful immigration policies, or progressives demanding answers from congressional Republicans at town halls in even the most conservative districts, it's clear that the 54 percent of us who voted against Donald Trump are ready to fight back. We just need a plan.

In a red state that Donald Trump won by 19 percent, I came within 3 percent of turning a Senate seat blue. And I didn't do it by hugging the middle and pretending to be a moderate Republican.

I'm proud that we took on some of the biggest names in Republican politics and darn near shocked the world. The chamber of commerce campaigned against me. Senator Ted Cruz swung by. Even Wayne LaPierre from the National Rifle Association showed up. But even after all of that, and despite the fact that I was the liberal kid from Kansas City who became well-known for supporting expanded background checks in a pro-gun state, I'm proud that we didn't back down. We demonstrated that the most important thing Democrats can do is make their argument and be authentic.

I told audiences that Black Lives Matter in Ferguson, but I did the same in rural areas. I stood up for an increase in the minimum wage no matter whether I was with underpaid janitors in Kansas City or a local chamber of commerce in a rural county. I talked about the value of organized labor whether I was in a union hall in St. Louis or a county fair four hours away. I made it clear why equal pay was important while at a Planned Parenthood event or talking to a reporter in a small town.

In each case, I've been unafraid to tell voters why lifting up strangers lifts them up too. They might not all agree with me every time, but they know I mean it and they know I care about everyone, including them.

The thing about telling the truth about what you believe is that it works. I learned this lesson when I ran for state representative in a three-way Democratic primary in 2008. I was twenty-six when I started running, and everybody said, "Nice young man, probably gonna come in a distant third." I knocked on a lot of doors in that race, so I don't remember all of them, but I remember this one, because it was one of the first.

I was already pretty nervous when the voter came to the door. He asked me about an issue and I gave him my opinion. It turned out he didn't agree with me. I didn't know any better, so I started doing what I'd seen politicians on TV do. I started trying to convince the voter that our two views weren't really different at all, trying to make my position sound like something he'd agree with.

From the look on this guy's face, it wasn't working, and I was starting to wonder if I'd made the right choice in running for office at all. Then I blurted out, "I guess you and I disagree on this, but I'm really trying to do what's best for everybody, so even if we don't agree, at least you'll know where I'm coming from."

To my surprise, he replied, "That's fair. I'll vote for you and you can put a sign in the yard." I became instantly addicted to carrying on an honest conversation with voters and knocked on twenty thousand doors in that race. With that approach, I won when no one thought I could.

As we Democrats consider the way forward as a party out of power, my humble suggestion is this: Let's start by being unafraid to make our argument to everyone. I'm not interested in conceding a single voter to the Republicans.

My experience as a progressive in a red state has taught me that voters will forgive you for disagreeing with them on an issue so long as they know you are genuine in your belief and that they are included in your vision for the country. Democrats need to get back to doing that again.

And that starts with us, the much-maligned Millennials. A new generation is stepping forward in America. Don't let anyone tell you that this generation is selfish. This is a generation that cares more about ideas than ideology and measures patriotism not by a politician's eagerness to go to war but by his or her willingness to do what's right, no matter the political cost.

And as the first-ever Millennial elected to statewide office in this nation, I'll have your back if you put yourself out there. So whether it's running for office, getting involved in your local community, or volunteering on a campaign, don't wait. The time to act is now. It's our time to take the lead and set the direction.

I'll see you out there.

Do Something

by Senator Cory Booker

U.S. senator from New Jersey | Mayor of Newark, New Jersey, 2006–13

■ **"I know what you should do.** Yup, I know exactly what you should do," said Ms. Virginia Jones, the elderly tenant leader of Newark's Brick Towers—a mentor, a friend, a neighbor, and in this moment, the last person I wanted to see on what had been my worst day in elected office thus far.

I was thirty years old, a year into my term as a city councilman representing Newark, New Jersey's Central Ward, and arriving home at the end of a day I had thought could be my last in politics.

The day had started with another unfortunate interaction with a friend and ally—the tenant leader of another building, Elaine Sewell. Elaine had called me early in the day to ask for my help—a violent incident had recently occurred at Garden Spires in which some guys involved in a drug trade had attacked the building security guards. Her buildings were similar to the ones Ms. Jones and I lived in, Brick Towers—twin brick structures with many units of low-income housing and a virulent drug trade too often marked by violence. Despite the challenges, the community was strong, with great families and senior citizens who embraced me and elected me to represent them in city hall.

When Elaine called and begged me to do something about this most recent incident, she didn't know that my first year as a councilman—what I had thought would be my opportunity to transform my ward and the city council—hadn't exactly gone as I thought it would. I had learned some tough lessons over the course of that year, and at the time of our conversation, I was still learning. Change is not easy. Political leaders, many of whom had been serving in the city for decades, didn't greet a young upstart reformer with enthusiasm. As I fought for change, I got a tremendous amount of pushback. And in Newark's machine politics, it often got ugly and frustrating. Even the press seemed to find my trials fascinating, and some of the challenges I faced were utterly surprising—from having my phones tapped to my car ticketed time and time again for parking where other city council people also parked.

So, toward the end of my first year in office, on that day I spoke to Elaine, not only did I feel boxed out by the political establishment and even a bit intimidated by what was thrown at me, I had also not passed a single meaningful bill; I hadn't made a lasting impact on the city, or even my ward. I was frustrated and even questioning why I got into politics. And then Elaine called me, asking for my help. I told her to call the mayor, to call the police. I couldn't even get the mayor to stop ticketing my car—how was I supposed to do anything about what was happening at Garden Spires?

Elaine was frustrated, and she retorted, "If you can't help, then why did we elect you?" Her exclamation cut me deeply, jabbing at my insecurities and adding fuel to my growing sense of failure.

I left my office in city hall that day angry, hurt, and actively considering altering my life path away from politics.

But when I arrived home to Brick Towers, I saw Ms. Jones.

I didn't particularly feel like talking, so I walked briskly and tried to pass her to get up to my apartment.

"Boy, don't you just walk past me," she said, and held out her arms for a hug. I obliged, and she demanded to know what was wrong. So I let her have it. I unloaded all of my frustrations, my conversation with Elaine, and my anger—at the dysfunction of the city government; at the tough, hardball-playing Mayor Sharpe James; at the other city council people; and more. I went on and on and on. Finally, after exclaiming more than once, I said, "I don't know what to do."

So Ms. Jones looked at me and said the words I had been waiting for: "I know what you should do."

I waited with bated breath for what seemed like an eternity for this wise and tough-loving elder to tell me what to do.

And finally she said with much enthusiasm, as if she were imparting her greatest wisdom upon me, "Cory, you should do . . . something."

She repeated, "You should do something."

It was a frustrating response that at first made me furious—"That's it!?"—but after cooling down for a while, I realized it was exactly what I needed to hear, and it's something I have carried with me since that day: the idea that we cannot let our inability to do everything undermine our determination to do something.

I was taught by my parents and my many mentors that a single act of kindness—something—no matter how small, has the ability and the power to shape history. They taught me that any success I found in life was in part because of generations of Americans who came before me, ordinary people with extraordinary courage who helped one another, stood up for one another, and loved one another. The collective small acts of these patriots have transformed the world in which we live. I was taught that the blessings I enjoy were made possible by regular folks who just kept on giving and serving and loving. I could not pay them back. But I could pay it forward.

I learned from my elders that if you want to see kindness in the world, be kind; if you want the world to be more hopeful, have hope; and don't expect the world to change if you are not willing to, every day, live the change yourself.

Alice Walker once said, "The most common way people give up their power is by thinking they don't have any." As Americans—no matter our title, our privilege, our income, our race, our gender, our sexual orientation, or our religion—we are endowed with a special ability and a special responsibility to do *something* to effect change in our country and make it better for the next generation of Americans.

We always have the ability to do something, no matter how small or seemingly insignificant; we always have the power to choose how to react to injustices in our own lives and in the lives of our neighbors. Injustices persist not just because of those who insidiously carry them out but because too many good people do nothing to end the injustice.

If you've decided that *something* means running for local office, do it. Do the thing you would do if you thought you could not fail. Don't be intimidated by the scale of the journey. Take it one day, one challenge, one step at a time. And no matter what the outcome, know that when you strike out for a cause or purpose greater than yourself, there is no loss. You will make a difference.

Find a community of people who will cheer you on and support you—you probably already have it. Think of neighbors, friends, and acquaintances—approach them for ideas, bring them on board with yours, talk about your inspiration and your enthusiasm.

Your courage will be contagious; your passion will be infectious.

Knock on doors, engage in conversations, and find people you disagree with—listen to them, really listen with a courageous empathy, and seek to understand them even more than you try to make yourself understood. We are all in this together—and we are all called to serve, to help, to encourage each other.

Above all, remember the incredible power you have as an individual to effect positive change in your neighborhood, your school, your community—to do something.

5
HOW TO RUN FOR OFFICE

■ **So! You've identified the problem** you want to solve and the office that lets you solve it. Now you're ready to run.

Start by reading through this section on what you need to know as you're planning out your race, and then dig into the three different components of a campaign: mobilization, message, and money (or, the three M's). I'll explain all the options you have for reaching voters, crafting your message, and raising money to fund your campaign.

I'm not going to tell you exactly what to do—that'd be both irresponsible and a bit condescending. There is no single right or wrong way to run a campaign. You've got some decisions to make as to how you want to run your race, keeping in mind your own community, the size of the election you're running in, your strengths and weaknesses, and what you actually have the time and capacity for. I want to make sure you know your options and understand the trade-offs of your decisions.

On page 155, you'll find a guide for a campaign plan. After wrapping your head around your race, put pen to paper (or fingers to keyboard) and commit to what you want to do.

As you read through this, remember that campaigns are like start-ups, with one simple goal: you need to talk to as many voters as possible before a specific deadline in order to win their vote. Everything you do—the team you hire, the money you raise and spend, the press you get—is geared toward that. If it's not directly related to that goal, you're doing the wrong thing.

TWELVE STEPS TO TAKE BEFORE YOU GET STARTED

Step One: Get to know the lay of the land.

You should know the details about your "community" (a word I'm using to mean the city, town, or legislative district you're trying to represent). Much of this is obvious, and you'll likely know the answers if you've grown up somewhere or lived somewhere for a few years, but it's worth taking a few minutes to think about these different categories:

- Demographics: How many people live in your community? What's the racial and gender breakdown of those people, how old are they, and how much money do they make?

- Geography: On a very basic level, what are the geographic boundaries of your community? Does that match up with the more organic ways communities organize themselves? (Electoral districts are sometimes drawn in such a way that it might not seem to be at all related to how people actually live—a boundary line might separate you and your next-door neighbor.)

- Economics: What is the primary industry in your community? What are the corporations and what are the small businesses that drive your local economy? What are the prices of goods like milk or eggs, and can people afford them? Is climate change fucking with local businesses?

- Housing: Where do people live and how much does it cost? What's the housing market like? Do people tend to grow up in your community and then stay there, or is it more transient?

- Health: Do people in your community have access to affordable health care? What's the uninsured rate? Where do women go for reproductive health care?

- Transportation: How do people get around? Is the public transit any good? Is it affordable? What kind of people use it? Is the traffic bad? Are the roads well maintained?

- Education: What are the various levels of schools available in your community? Are they any good? Think about everything, from preschool through higher education.

- Culture: What do people do for fun in your community? Are there sports teams (and do people care)? What is the local hot spot on a Friday night? How about on a Tuesday afternoon? Is there a community center? Are there museums? Is there theater? Is there a music scene? Where do people tend to gather? What about restaurants? What are the big events for the community?

- Community: What are the different civic organizations where you live? Consider religious entities, nonprofits, political parties, and unions—all different "groups" people can be members of.

- Government: If you're going to run for a government position, make sure you know how the government works.

- Communications: Where do people in your community get their news? Who are the influential reporters in the area? How about the influential social media users? Are there local news channels? Do people watch them? What's the local radio station, and who listens to it?

- Assumptions: What are the stereotypes of your community? Be tough but fair; ask yourself if those stereotypes have any basis in reality. What are the values your community upholds? (For example: Is your town inclusive? Does it encourage diversity or try to stamp it out?)

- Vocabulary: Do people in your community say "soda," "pop," or just "Coke"? Is it a "traffic circle" or a "roundabout"? Don't overthink this—be authentically you!—but being aware of the local lingo is important.

■ Tip No. 1: Pretend you're visiting your community for the first time as a tourist and want to do research ahead of your visit. Websites like TripAdvisor or Yelp can illuminate what people care about.

Tip No. 2: You're going to think you know the whole lay of the land of your community (or at least have a general sense of the vibe) but you should confirm what you know. Wikipedia might not be a good source for academic research, but it's a great place to gut-check your instincts and get some basic numbers. Enjoy the internet wormhole you're about to go down.

As you're thinking about this research, acknowledge your own blind spots. A straight African American woman navigates a community in a different way than a gay Latino man, who in turn has a different experience than a white woman, for example. Your personal experience in your community is what makes you a valuable addition to representative democracy, but not all of the citizens you're aiming to represent will see the world in the same way.

Push yourself out of your comfort zone and don't be afraid to acknowledge your privilege, what you know, and what you don't. If you think there's a part of your community you don't have access to because of who you are, seek out someone who can help you learn it.

Step Two: Do your political due diligence.

Knowing the economic and cultural landscape of your community is important, but the political landscape is a different beast all together. This is likely the kind of assessment you haven't made before (because, honestly, why would you?) and you might not know the answers off the top of your head. Here's what to investigate.

The Local Party Players Find the local Democratic committee or party in your district and check out their website. If they have an office in your district, stop by and see who's there. There's probably a leadership structure—usually it includes titles like "chair" or "precinct captain." Do some research online to figure out who these folks are and what their backgrounds are.

Know the names of the elected officials who represent your community at every level—your senators, members of Congress, statewide officials, and the locals. Often the highest-level elected official from your state is considered the de facto head of the party, but that's not always true. You can find out all of this information on the state Democratic party website.

■ Most "political research" should look a little like what you probably do before you go on a first date with a stranger from the internet. Google him or her; check out Facebook, Twitter, and LinkedIn; read any news articles; and maybe watch a few videos. Check out his or her friends, get to know his or her network, and see if you have anyone or thing in common. I'm not going to pretend this isn't a little weird—it totally is—but it's also how you prep to make political connections (and how you make sure you don't go on a date with a serial killer).

A Note About Navigating the Professional Political Landscape When you start to dig in and identify who you need to talk to, you're going to discover that politics and government are like any other workplace. There are people who are nominally in charge based on titles, elections, and promotions. Then there are people who actually get things done. Those two categories might overlap but often they don't.

To be "good at politics" means to know where the real power centers are, what their interests are, and how to get aligned with—or strategically against—them to get something done. This is where politics gets fun (or fucked up, depending on your point of view): Workplace dynamics in politics and government can have a serious impact on policy and, accordingly, on the lives of millions of people. The stakes are high.

In some workplaces, you can get away with being good at your job without actually liking your coworkers. In politics, that's just not true. You need to be popular with the voters to win, *and* you need to be popular with your peers—the network of elected officials and professionals who will support you both in campaigning and governing—to get anything meaningful done.

The two groups act as counterbalances on each other. A politician who's popular with the voters will have more job security and more "political capital" to throw around; a politician who's popular with his or her peers will have more resources to get things done for constituents and to reinforce his or her campaign.

Your most important currency in politics is your relationships with others. This reliance on transactional relationships is one of the many reasons why people often hate politicians and government. The "game" can make people heartless and soulless. It tends to reward a particular kind of narcissistic manipulator who can succeed by using other people's feelings, egos, and ambitions in order to satisfy their own goals and ascend through the ranks.

But it doesn't have to be this way. The only way to change the "game" is to change the players. That starts with you. Be the kind of politician you'd want to be represented by: someone motivated by doing good for people, whose intentions are founded in values and not ego. You're not running because you want to be famous, glamorous, or occupy a corner office. You're running because you see a problem that needs to be solved. You're in it for the right reasons and the good news is that there are enough people like you, especially on the local level, who will become your allies.

Much of navigating the local political network is on you—you'll need to have good emotional intelligence and a nose for bullshit. Realistically, I can't coach you through that in a few pages of a book. (I suggest a good therapist to start.) But if you're going to be a good member of the world of professional politics, a few tips:

- Don't take anything personally. Most people, both in politics and in the "real" world, are relatively self-absorbed—they're not going out of their way to hurt or insult you; they just didn't think of you in the first place.

- Take responsibility when you fuck up; be forgiving when other people do the same.

- Asking someone for help or advice is a way of showing them you value their brain and experience. It requires you to swallow your ego. Do it anyway.

- Lift people up. Is someone doing great work? Shout it from the rooftops. You're only as good as your network; make sure people know how great your friends and colleagues are. (Google "Shine Theory" + "Ann Friedman" + "Aminatou Sow" for more.)

I repeat: Try to be the kind of politician (and person) you'd want to vote for.

All that being said: To succeed in this system and eventually change it, you need to start by working within it.

So, back to the task at hand: getting to know the local political players. To actually do this, you need to show up in person wherever you think they'll be. That might mean volunteering for local campaigns or coming out to happy hours, fundraisers, town halls, or rallies. Follow the local party on Facebook and Twitter, and follow the individuals—they'll likely be sharing these events on social media.

Show up, be helpful, and talk to people. This isn't complicated; treat it like any other normal social encounter. Ask questions and be actively interested in the answers. Keep showing up.

You'll get to know people through repeated proximity and similar interests. Make sure to seek out the people behind the scenes—the ones in the back of the room, organizing volunteers or signing in folks. Those are the real doers. They'll give you the scoop on who actually matters and will be able to help you navigate the waters of your community's politics.

A **political action committee (PAC)** is an organization that collects money and then donates it to a political cause or candidate. Some PACs are organized around ideologies or demographics; others are organized around trade groups or specific issues. For example, there are PACs that just give to young women, or LGBTQ candidates, or people who run on a platform of climate change or support a specific union's policies. Donations to PACs and contribution limits to PACs vary from state to state. Some people choose not to take PAC money—that's your call as a candidate.

A **super PAC** is an "independent-expenditure-only committee" that can raise and spend unlimited amounts of money but cannot directly donate to a campaign. The Supreme Court made super PACs possible through their decision in *Citizens United v. FEC* in 2010, opening the door to a flood of money from corporations, individuals, and unions. There are easily thousands of think pieces online about the effect super PACs have had on politics, if that's your thing. What you need to know as a candidate is that, in most states, you legally cannot coordinate with super PACs, so check with a lawyer.

Labor unions get involved in politics as a way of advocating for legislation and policies that benefit their members. Unions are big in local politics in part because their members are prolific volunteers. Getting a union's support can mean both money and volunteer efforts.

"Special interest" is an umbrella term used to mean anything from an advocacy group to a lobbying organization. Some special-interest groups are extraordinarily powerful and can mobilize massive amounts of money and volunteers when they get involved (think: the NRA on the right and Planned Parenthood on the left). Getting an endorsement from one of these groups helps your campaign financially and also lends it some credibility.

Knowing the relevant players in these groups is part of doing your political due diligence. Try and find old campaign literature from past races for the same office to get a sense of which organizations "play" in your kind of election. You can also look at old campaign finance reports, which will show you which groups donated money.

Before you announce your candidacy, meet with these people and let them know you're thinking about running—and ask them for their support. Send them handwritten thank-you notes afterward. It'll mean a lot.

■ To "play" in a race means to endorse one of the candidates and, accordingly, give money and credibility. Try not to get nauseated by the fact that professional politicos use the word "play" to describe a process that involves huge sums of money changing hands and having a massive impact on people's lives.

> "*The best campaign advice I ever got was, 'Run like you're ten points down.' It keeps you on your game, and it keeps you sharp. In August, public polling had me at 7 percent. I could have given up there. I could have decided to go outside of the plan. Instead, I stuck to the plan, and on November 8, I won outright.*"
>
> —LEVAR STONEY, mayor of Richmond, VA, on why you should know the stats (and then ignore them)

Step Three: Learn the stats.

Take a look at the election results for the last five elections at every level and get familiar with the patterns in turnout and results.

Results for a presidential race are *not* indicative of what you should expect for your race but can be a helpful baseline for where your district might fall on the partisan spectrum.

Head to CookPolitical.com to look up the Cook Partisan Voting Index (PVI) for your congressional district. This is a number calculated by comparing how your district voted relative to the country as a whole during the last two presidential elections. A PVI of "D+5" means that the district's voter spread resulted in an average of five points more Democratic than the national spread. This number is mostly meaningless for anyone not working at the DCCC or a congressional race, but reporters sometimes use it to describe a district, so understanding what it means can be useful.

LEARN MORE ON THE INTERNET Google "[THE POSITION YOU'RE RUNNING FOR]" + "[YOUR CITY]" + "election" + "results." You should be able to find an official .gov website or news source that lays out the results. Ballotpedia.org does a great job of collecting local election data, depending on where you live and what race you're looking at.

Step Four: Figure out your win number.

Your win number is exactly what it sounds like: the number of votes you'll likely need to win. In most races, that number is often called your "50+1", meaning 50 percent of the votes cast plus one to get you the majority. If you're in a multi-candidate race or a primary (or in a state like Louisiana or California, with "jungle primaries" where the top two finishers go on to the general election regardless of party), your win number might be a different percentage of the total.

Using the same Google search as above, track down the total number of registered voters in your community and use past similar-size elections as a way to predict how many voters will turn out in your election.

For example: You're running for city council against one other candidate. There are ten thousand registered voters in your community. In the last three city council races over the past decade, turnout sadly hovered in the 10 percent range. Once, it jumped to 18 percent, but that was an anomaly—a town celebrity was running and spent a lot of money. Based on that history, you can expect about one thousand people to come vote in your election, but you're going to be conservative, bump that number up a little bit, and hope that 1,150 come out to vote. Divide that in half, add one, and your win number is 576.

If the information is available, you can find breakdowns by neighborhood and figure out your vote goals on an even more detailed level. That's helpful for understanding how to prioritize your time and money.

Sometimes the math can get more complicated, especially if there hasn't been a contested race for the position you're running for in a while, or if you're running against someone in a primary. But none of this is calculus; you can figure it out with simple calculations.

Step Five: Do some math and calculate how much it costs to run.

There isn't a one-race or one-seat-fits-all answer to the question of how much money you need. A school board race might cost $1,000 and a state assembly race might cost $250,000 (or $1 million). To figure out a baseline, review past campaign finance reports.

> LEARN MORE ON THE INTERNET Google "[OFFICE YOU'RE RUNNING FOR]" + "[YOUR CITY/STATE]" + "campaign finance report." This will probably take you to the same place where you'll find finance rules and other campaign requirements for your position: the website of the board, division, or commission that oversees elections in your jurisdiction.

Campaign finance rules and disclosure laws vary from state to state, but generally speaking, you should be able to find the total amount the campaign raised and how much they spent—and usually some information about what they spent it on.

Take a look at the most recent election data, as well as the data from the last time there was a competitive, close race. If there hasn't been a competitive race in a few cycles, look up similar-size races in geographically adjacent districts.

You're trying to get a sense of how much field and media operations tend to cost for races in your area with your media market.

You can use those numbers plus the turnout numbers to figure out how much the past campaigns spent per vote. This is helpful directional info as you begin to flesh out your own budget.

Outside groups may also spend money to influence the race. You can learn which ones have gotten involved before by reading old newsclips about past elections.

Step Six: Figure out how to actually get your name on the ballot.

The rules for filing are set either by the state or the political party within the state, and vary from place to place.

You might simply need to pay a filing fee that might be a set amount or the percentage of the salary that office earns. You might need to get a certain number of signatures on a particular kind of petition. You might need to do both. The political parties can also set their own rules for how you earn their nomination; it might be via a caucus or a convention process, or it might be through a nominating process.

It's a clusterfuck. However, it's one you can navigate.

Call your city clerk. Ask for the guide for candidates running for office. Nearly every election administrator has a guide for candidates—if you stop by in person, they'll even give you a paper version. You can get a copy of all the filing documents and required campaign reports, and you might even be able to get a manual of election laws that will apply to your campaign.

Other things you can ask for while you've got them on the phone:

▪ A map of your district

▪ The political calendar for the year

▪ Any campaign manuals they have on hand

- The voter file (Jump to page 96 for more details on what the voter file is and how you'll use it.)

- A list of other filed candidates

- Contact information for who you should reach out to with questions about campaign finance rules and regulations

You absolutely should not hesitate to pick up the phone (or, more realistically, open your Gmail and type up an email) to reach out to past candidates. Find them on Facebook or Twitter and direct-message them—ask them if you can chat about their campaign operations. Pick their brains about their budgets, what they wish they'd done differently, and what they think went well. Even if they lost, they'll have some valuable takeaways.

Step Seven: Plan your campaign structure.

> "*My campaign manager was twenty-two, my field director was twenty-one, and my communications director was twenty. It was a true youth effort. This was a real insurgency. The entire strategy for my campaign was going door to door. As the youngest candidate, people weren't going to take me seriously unless they had a chance to meet me and ask me every question under the sun so they could gain enough confidence to support the campaign. My goal was to knock on every door in the city once. After I did that, our internal tracking showed that we were still behind, so I quit my job, lived off my savings for a bit, and knocked on every door in the city two and a half times. By going door to door, you meet people who become volunteers, who go out and knock on doors themselves. That's entirely how we won.*"

—SVANTE MYRICK, mayor of Ithaca, on how he built his campaign team

No candidate is an island—you're going to need an organization to help you run and win. But forget about what you've seen on TV about presidential campaigns, or even the big staffs that come with gubernatorial or congressional races. Your race will likely have one person on staff, maybe two if you're rolling in the money. That's okay! (Head to page 197 to see the kinds of variations on campaign structures if you're thinking about working for one instead of running yourself.)

As you think about your team, consider that even the most bare-bones campaign structure will require a few key positions.

Campaign Manager This is the most senior person on your team after you. This person has to be a jack- or jane-of-all-trades. If you can pay him or her, you should. Your campaign manager is the CEO of your team. Find someone you trust: He or she should be able to talk to the media on your behalf, help with fundraising, manage volunteers, and make sure everyone else working with your campaign is doing their damn job. S/he'll be coordinating allies, driving strategy, and making key spending decisions. Choose wisely.

How to find a campaign manager:

- Ask around. Email prior candidates who ran for this office and ask them who managed their campaigns.

- Try the state or local party. Sometimes they've got résumé banks; other times they have longtime volunteers who can take on the job.

- Find the contact information for your local Young Democrats or College Democrats branch. A young, scrappy upstart who cares about politics could be just what you need.

Know who has the final say on any given decision— you or your campaign manager. This seems silly, but

> ■ It might be easy to ask a family member or your significant other to be your campaign manager, but consider finding someone without the kind of fraught baggage that comes with those relationships. What you really want is someone who will tell it to you straight. Don't bring on someone who will just tell you want they think you want to hear; bring on someone to offer up their judgment and challenge your thinking where appropriate.

you need to know who the buck stops with. Ideally, you've picked a campaign manager you trust to make decisions on your behalf.

Expect to be talking to this person every day, all day long. You'll be in constant communication, so pick someone you like.

Treasurer (Sometimes Called Finance Director, Fundraising Director, Development Director) This is someone who will keep track of all the money in and money out. Often they're responsible for the mechanics of fundraising and following up with donors. They're the ones who will file all the paperwork with the local election administrators and make sure you don't get fined for breaking the law. Pick someone you trust who's good with paperwork AND people.

If you're building a bigger campaign, your next round of hiring might include positions like . . .

Communications Director (Sometimes Called Media, Public Relations, or Press Secretary) This is someone who can oversee all your communication with the press and voters. They'll do things like send press releases, pitch reporters, handle inquiries, and guide you with telling your story to voters and reporters. They also might oversee social media. They'll coach you through your message and overarching strategy on how you talk about your candidacy.

Digital Director Your campaign will have a website and a social media presence, because in the twenty-first century, if it's not online, it doesn't exist. You can decide whether or not your website is run by a separate "department," but you should have someone in charge of your online presence and what you're doing online to recruit volunteers, raise money, and talk to voters and reporters. If your digital and communications work are split between two members of your team, make sure they work well together.

Organizing Director (Sometimes Called Field Director, Volunteer Coordinator, or Manager) This person is in charge of scheduling, training, and overseeing volunteers. You're going to need volunteers—and you'll need structure in order to manage them.

We're not talking about overseeing thousands of people. But if you're passionate enough and compelling enough, you'll have a decent-size group of your friends, family, and people who are invested in your campaign who want to actually do something to help you—and once you step up to run and start talking about why you're running, you'll be surprised how many people are willing to lend a hand if you give them concrete tasks and show them how their work matters.

Build out a management structure. Once you've identified the voter-contact tactics you're going to employ (more on that to come) and how many people you need to reach, your organizing director should write up some "volunteer job descriptions" of tasks people can help you with.

Give people titles as much as you can—it's a way of both giving them responsibility and of holding them accountable. If you deputize someone as your "phone-bank captain," they'll brag about it to their friends and maybe put it on their résumé. They'll also take the responsibility of organizing your phone banks seriously, because it's their job.

Take care of your volunteers. Make sure they feel appreciated—that's as simple as saying thank you every time they do something for you. If you can afford it, pizza is always good for late nights at the office. If you've got the kind of volunteers who might appreciate it (and are old enough, of course), beer or wine is also usually welcome. If you've got volunteer leaders, do random acts of kindness for them. Flowers are a cheap but lovely way to show gratitude. Send thank-you notes constantly.

People start volunteering on a campaign for the candidate and the cause. They stay for the other people. Make sure your campaign culture is a good one by being a good, positive, friendly leader. Set the tone: No negativity. No complaining in front of your volunteers, and no bitching or moaning. What you're doing is hard, scary, and also an incredible privilege—you're getting a platform and a chance to make a difference in your community. Don't forget that.

You have a responsibility as a candidate to build something sustainable—the better you treat your volunteers, the more you build interest in helping future campaigns and cultivate potential candidates for office. Win or lose, you're going to need these folks to want to help you again if you decide to run (or to help other candidates in your area). Even someone doing the bare minimum to help is doing *something*, which is better than nothing. You and your organizing director will help set the tone for that.

Other leadership positions might include roles like . . .

GOTV (Get-Out-the-Vote) Director In a bigger campaign, you might have someone in charge of GOTV. If you're running a big operation, you'll need someone to be a bit removed from the day-to-day churn of the organization, and instead exclusively thinking and planning for the final stretch of the race when your only focus is literally people casting ballots. Your GOTV director might be in charge of things like absentee-ballot programs, early-vote programs, poll watchers, volunteer schedules for Election Day, literature distribution on Election Day, and the like.

Political Director Your political director will handle the politics of your campaign—working with elected officials, outside groups, and the various constituency organizations you might interact with. This should be someone who's well versed in the relationship dynamics of the district. They should know the party leaders and, more important, the staff that will help you actually get a meeting with the right people. This person should be patient and be willing to get yelled at on your behalf.

Policy Director This is the wonk of your campaign team—the person who gets a thrill out of sifting through city council proposals and reading or writing sample legislation. Your policy director will help you figure out exactly what you'd do as an elected official and how to get in the weeds (meaning: into the details). These people are often lawyers or trained economists. Even in a bigger race, you don't have to worry if you don't have a policy director; it's a nice-to-have staffer, not a need-to-have. You can also turn to your smart friends or people you meet on the trail and form a volunteer advisory council to help you think through positions and advise you.

Data Director (Sometimes Called Voter File Manager or Database Coordinator) As your volunteer structure and voter contact organization grows, you're going to want someone responsible for keeping track of all the various sources of information, making sure your voter file stays up to date, and creating lists for volunteers (and for you) to use when you're making calls or canvassing. Think of your nerdiest friend who loves Excel formulas and writes SQL code in their spare time. They can learn how to manage the voter file.

Step Eight: Find training for you and your team.

Seek out staff training so your folks can get the skills they need to be successful.

LEARN MORE ON THE INTERNET Google "political campaign staff" + "training" + "[YEAR OF ELECTION]" + "[YOUR STATE]."

Democrats might find training through organizations like Camp Wellstone or the Progressive Change Campaign Committee; Republicans might find them through the Leadership Institute. You should call up your state party and ask for recommendations for staff training. You can also try the affiliated committee for the office you're running for. Trainings sometimes have fees, but usually there are scholarships available, so money shouldn't ever get in the way if you really want to go.

There are also candidate trainings and boot camps.

LEARN MORE ON THE INTERNET Google "candidate training" + "[YOUR STATE]" + "[YOUR PARTY]."

Those same organizations listed for staff also do candidate trainings, as do groups like EMILY's List, the Victory Institute, and more. In the wake of the 2016 presidential election, tons of groups sprang up to train the flood of candidates who stepped up to run. If you head to runforsomething.net and sign up, we've got a complete list of groups on the progressive side who can walk you through a campaign. Particularly if you're a progressive woman or person of color, there are numerous organizations that will help you (and only you, or people like you) if you seek them out.

Step Nine: Get your Rolodex in order.

Start making lists of everyone you know. Export your phone contacts and email contacts, then set up a spreadsheet and merge everything together. Go through your Facebook friends and add them to the list as you feel comfortable, and do the same with your LinkedIn and Twitter connections. Any social media platform you're on is fair game.

Once you launch your campaign, everyone you have a personal connection to should be contacted in whatever way makes sense for them, and then followed up with again and again. These are the people you should be able to turn to first as supporters, then as volunteers or donors.

Step Ten: Write a campaign budget.

You have no guarantee regarding how much money you will raise. But you've got to start somewhere, so take the research you've done on how much past elections like yours usually cost and examine the finance reports to see what past candidates spent and where they spent it.

Keep your overhead costs low and think about where you can cut costs. You probably don't need to rent an entire office—if you need a campaign HQ, ask the local party if you can share their offices or reach out to other local candidates and see if you can go in on somewhere together. You could also just use your home if you have the space, or a friend's home or garage. You could even consider a coworking space if it's affordable and prevalent in your town. Any office space costs more than just rent; you'll also have to pay for utilities, supplies, furniture, and possibly insurance. Those costs can quickly add up.

When looking at other possible expenses, ask your state party if they have deals with local printers or mail houses that you can take advantage of. Be thrifty. Ask yourself with every expense: Does this actually get me in front of more voters? Or does it just make me feel like I'm doing something?

Before you spend a dime, a few questions to ask yourself . . .

- **How much will it actually cost? Don't let unit pricing fool you.**

- **How many voters will it actually reach?**

- **Is this a dumb idea? Does it seem like a trick? It's probably a trick.**

- **Will I be embarrassed when my campaign finance report shows I spent money on this? Think: fancy dinners or salaries for my family members.**

- **Can I get this for free? (And if I do find it for free, do I have to declare it as an in-kind donation on my campaign finance reports?)**

Step Eleven: Set up good operating systems.

Decide from the get-go that you won't fuck up when it comes to campaign finance. Your campaign funds should not be used for personal expenses. Don't use them to pay your rent, or buy video games, or cover new clothes for you. That's not just shitty to your donors; it's also likely illegal.

After you've filed with the appropriate administrator, open a separate bank account for your campaign. Get a separate charge card and checks, and keep a very clear record of where money comes from and where it's going. Generally speaking, you can't use personal funds to pay for campaign expenses without it either being reported as (A) a loan to your campaign or (B) an in-kind donation to your campaign. Getting dinged in campaign finance law violations is bad for your campaign's success and can ultimately be pretty expensive; often the penalty comes in the form of fines. If you fuck up badly enough, you could be disqualified from running at all or even end up in jail. (That's the most extreme consequence. But it could happen.)

Know exactly when and how you have to file campaign finance reports. You may have to disclose every donor; you may have to disclose only donors who contribute more than a certain amount. You might have to file every quarter, or it might be every week, or, leading up to Election Day, it might be every twenty-four or forty-eight hours. Know the rules and follow them. If you don't, the attack ads write themselves: "Candidate X can't be trusted to campaign responsibly. How can you trust Candidate X to govern responsibly?"

Figure out who you can ask legal questions of. Your state party might have a lawyer on retainer you can call on, or you might have friends with law degrees who can donate their time. Don't make any unforced legal errors.

Campaign finance laws might make your life a bit harder, but they are ultimately very good things. These laws exist to ensure that voters know how politicians get their money and how they spend it. The transparency enabled by campaign finance reports help protect the public from corruption.

Step Twelve: Get good photos taken.

If you're on any professional listservs, email around asking for a cheap photographer, or post about your search on Facebook. I've been shocked at how many people have an amateur interest in photography and will take professional headshots for you if you're willing to pay even a little bit.

Women, go get your hair blown out and stop by Sephora or MAC for a free-ish makeover before you get photos taken. Men, do whatever it is you do.

These photos will go everywhere: On your campaign materials, on your website, on news articles, and on anything partner organizations put out. Look your best.

Running a Campaign: Tips from an Expert

by Jen O'Malley Dillon

Partner at Precision Strategies | Deputy campaign manager
for President Barack Obama's 2012 campaign

■ **There is no magic in running campaigns,** just preparation and hard work. Campaigns may seem scary or overwhelming, making you believe that only an experienced professional knows how to run a campaign and that you can't do it without money and professional support behind you. But that is not true.

You can do this. And you don't need to be a millionaire, surrounded by a fleet of consultants to win.

Every single campaign is different, because a campaign is a reflection of the candidate, the position, the time, the community—there is no cookie-cutter approach to winning campaigns. We always say that if we had run the same playbook in 2012 for President Obama that we did in 2008, we would have lost.

There is no one way to run a winning campaign, but there is one way to run your campaign—and that is to customize it to you. Here are a few tips to keep in mind.

1. The most valuable things you have are money and time. And you will never have enough. Your entire campaign needs to be built efficiently and effectively using your resources and time. Don't let this paralyze you in the decision-making process. You simply need to make sure you understand your role and maximize your time doing the things only you can and should do.

2. Put your plan on paper—it's not a plan if it isn't written down. So much of the campaign will function in the moment, whether it is around a debate, a news piece, or a specific activity. One of the hardest parts of running a campaign is ensuring that all those day-to-day elements drive toward the broader goal and strategy. The absolute best way to ensure this is to have a plan written down on paper and refer to it on a regular basis, guaranteeing that your campaign is on track and focused on the long game.

3. Know why you are running and tell everyone you can. Your rationale for running and what you will do when elected are the most important stories you can tell, whether you are talking to voters, supporters, donors, organizations, or the press.

   - Your voice is critical, but you alone cannot carry your message. You will need the help of your campaign, supporters, surrogates, and other voters to reach beyond your networks to share your message.

   - You'll get sick of hearing yourself saying the same thing, but that's just when you'll start to break through.

   - Make it easy for people to know why you are running and what you will do when elected—verbally and in writing.

   - Maintain the same message frame no matter what audience you are talking to, and communicate on issues through the broader message lens outlined through your campaign.

   - Don't just tell people what you bring to the table—show them! You should be able to demonstrate your commitment, energy, and passion for public service.

4. Surround yourself with people you trust who can help you. You cannot and should not run your campaign alone. You need to be a candidate, not a campaign manager, and a campaign is a pretty large operation, even for a local race.

   - If you can afford to hire a professional campaign team, do it! But if you can't, find the people in your life who know you and can help you, and give them a role.

- Look for people whom you trust and who will give you honest feedback. You will be a better candidate and operate a better campaign if you are surrounded by people who can both support you and help you make the tough choices.

- Find people who are organized, who are good with social media, who can put together a database, who don't mind speaking at events, and who are good at organizing events. If you look closely within your own network, you can find people who excel at each of these things. Look to your family, friends, and colleagues.

5. Understand your path to victory. As a candidate and as the person who is ultimately responsible for your campaign, you need to know what it will take to win, and then you need a plan that helps you do that.

  - Your path to victory is the path that gets you to a win number. In a two-person race, we often say that is 50 percent plus one.

  - This is not always an exact science. You need to spend some time understanding what has historically happened in your race to compile the best assessment of what will happen in your race. That means you need to look at and understand several factors:

    - *Total turnout numbers (numbers of people who voted)*

    - *Breakout by partisanship if available (Democrat, Republican, independent/unaffiliated)*

    - *How voting is conducted (in-person on Election Day, early, absentee)*

    - *How many candidates are in the race and guidelines results*

    - *What other atmospherics might influence the overall election (enthusiasm for election, timing, other issues on ballot, debates, etc.)*

  - Once you understand your district by the numbers, there are only three ways to reach a winning scenario:

    - *Getting Out the Vote: By making sure the voters that support you turn out to vote.*

- *Voter Registration: By finding new people to vote and add to the pool of supporters.*

- *Persuasion: By converting undecided or swing voters into your supporters.*

- Every campaign's path to victory is created by a mix of GOTV, voter registration, and persuasion.

- Your campaign's right mix should use an estimation of turnout as a base and then build on voter registration and persuasion as needed to get to your win number.

- Most campaigns require some of each of these three programs but the balance is not equal—your unique district and race will help determine what you need to build to win.

6. Build your campaign organization over time. One of the most important elements of a campaign that is often overlooked is capacity building—creating a campaign foundation that allows you to grow and scale when it matters most—during the final weeks leading up to the election.

   - You do not have to have every piece of your campaign plan, staff, and strategy in place the day you announce your candidacy. Some of the pieces will take some time to refine and pull together.

   - The most important thing you can do is build a foundation of your campaign so it is ready to scale for the final weeks of the campaign—this includes having the most activity, empowering the operation to reach the most voters, and conveying the most effective messaging to the right audiences.

7. Reach as many voters as directly as you can. Winning campaigns create more opportunities for the candidate to get in front of voters to make their case, to ask for their support, and to ask for their help.

   - As a candidate, you are asking people for one of the most personal things they can give: their vote. You need to work for it and earn it.

   - Make sure you build your campaign to put you in front of as many voters as possible.

- You can't win if you don't ask!

- Don't stop at just asking for their vote. Ask your supporters to talk to their own networks, sharing why they're supporting you and asking those in their network to do the same thing.

8. Get Out the Vote (GOTV). The ten days before the election are the most critical to ensure your supporters are turning out to vote for you.

   - It is not enough to just get a voter to say they are with you. You need to make sure that they translate that support into an actual vote for you.

   - That means you should track voters who are with you, including their contact information, so that you can follow up with them before the election.

   - You need to ensure that they have all the information they need to vote for you, including the details on where they vote, what they need to have with them (this varies by state), and when the polls are open.

   - In 2002, I worked on South Dakota senator Tim Johnson's reelection and we won statewide by a 524-vote margin of victory. Every door knocked on, every phone call, reminder, and conversation in those final days mattered.

So, let's start where we began: Building and executing successful campaigns is not magic. It just takes preparation and hard work. You can do this!

6
MOBILIZATION
(OR, HOW YOU REACH VOTERS)

■ **You've decided to run for office,** done your political due diligence, and determined how you might build your team—now your singular goal is to talk to as many people as possible to make sure they vote for you on or before Election Day. Anything that doesn't directly connect to that goal is a waste of your time and money.

The umbrella term for this work is "voter contact"—it should encompass everything your campaign does, from canvassing to advertising online to utilizing social media. Each method of communicating with voters is a tactic. Your campaign's overall strategy is made up of piecing together these tactics, deciding which of them to use to connect with a particular voter, and then deciding what to say to that voter once you've gotten his or her attention.

I'll break each tactic down into its building blocks and explain how you, the candidate, might execute on it. When you sit down to write your campaign plan (which, again, you have to do because if it's not written down, it won't happen), keep in mind: You're not going to be able to do everything. You're going to have to prioritize which tactics are most important to you with which groups of voters. You'll have to decide what is a good use of your time, what you can plug volunteers into, and what you can afford to pay people to do.

None of these actions happen in a silo. Ideally, every voter you need to connect with will get "touched" (meaning: talked to—no actual touching; you're not Donald Trump) multiple times. The dream is that they'll hear from you so much they'll get sick of you. (That probably won't happen. In your race, you won't be saturating the market the way a presidential campaign does.) People don't decide not to vote because they hear from a campaign too many times, even if they might threaten to.

Start with a basic question: Which people should your campaign talk to?

To figure that out, you need to look at the voter file. What the fuck is a voter file, you ask? Good question.

Who someone voted for is always private. Whether or not someone voted at all, however, is public. All that information is found in a database called "the voter file." Back in the old days (meaning before the late 1990s), voter files were literally filing cabinets with boxes of index cards listing people's voting records. Now it's a computer database.

There are multiple voter files—the official one is kept by secretaries of state around the country; each includes a list of every registered voter, their address of registration, party affiliation if the state requires it, and basic voting history (i.e., they voted in 2004 and 2008 but not the elections in between).

Each national committee—in coordination with state parties—keeps its own record of the voter file. These databases include all of the official information from election administrators, which is then combined with everything else a political campaign might know about a voter: donation history, email address, phone number, volunteer efforts, outreach, race, ethnicity, occupation, and often consumer data purchased through outside vendors.

There are also a few corporations that keep updated voter files. The Koch brothers fund one that keeps a Republican registry; on the Democratic side, there are groups like Catalist and TargetSmart that keep voter files up to date for campaigns to access.

A "good" voter file is one that is regularly updated and thorough. Its data is "clean" (meaning: easily sortable) and refreshed each cycle. State and local campaigns are the ones actually doing this work by talking to voters and filling in the information.

There is no shortcut here: A volunteer literally calls a voter or knocks on their door, asks them a few questions, and records their answers, which get entered into a database. Every single event your campaign puts on should include data collection—there should be a sign-in sheet of some kind, whether paper or on a computer or tablet. Every piece of information helps your campaign refine your list of voters you can count on to show up, voters who might be persuadable, and voter who are likely a lost cause.

If your election has early voting or absentee voting, your voter file will ideally show you which people have already cast their ballots, often in the form of daily updates. While you won't know with 100 percent certainty whether or not they voted for you, you can make a pretty good guess based on their party affiliation, their voting history, and your own campaign's contact with them. Once they've voted, you can cross them off your list of people to talk to.

The voter file will become your bible, because your campaign has two limited resources: time and money. Every choice you make is about balancing those two resources and making sure you're being strategic, efficient, and effective. The voter file will be your be-all and end-all list for deciding which voters to talk to and when.

■ Hot tip: If you're just a voter and not a candidate, one of the best ways to stop getting calls from a campaign is simply to vote as early as you're legally allowed to.

HOW TO ACTUALLY GET A COPY OF THE VOTER FILE

You've got a few options here:

1. Check your secretary of state's website. In many states, you can literally download a CSV file of your local voter file for free. In other states, you might have to pay a fee. Some places might mail you a CD-ROM (seriously . . .); others might give you paperwork. This will give you baseline voter info without all the bonus features of the party's work; it likely won't include software to manage the information, so keep that in mind.

2. Reach out to your state party. Some state parties will give access to the coordinated voter file to any Democrat running; others might limit it during a primary and won't give folks access until the general election. Some might charge candidates a small rental or licensing fee. On the Democratic side, the party might ask you to pay for access to a tool called NGP VAN—this is software used to access the voter file and then create lists of voters to talk to. As of writing, NGP VAN has a monopoly in the party—it's the only game in town for accessing the consolidated, official Democratic Party voter file. That will hopefully change over time.

3. NationBuilder, and similar services, will provide local races with the voter file free of charge. While this version of the voter file won't have the compounded data from years of Democratic campaigns inputting information, it's a baseline to start from.

    LEARN MORE ON THE INTERNET Google "[YOUR CITY]" + "voter file."

Whatever way you get access to it, make sure you keep your voter file in a way that is accessible to your team. Some campaigns have an expression: "If it's not in the VAN, it doesn't exist." (VAN being a reference to NGP VAN.) If you don't track your voter contact, the information gathered doesn't matter, because you can't do anything with it.

The voter file you get likely won't include many, if any, online interactions. In an ideal world, you'd be able to consolidate all your interactions with a voter into a single database, creating a 360-degree view of a voter. You'd know if you knocked on their door, if they came to a rally, if you emailed them, if they donated, if they tweeted at you—you'd be able to track everything and use that to inform how you reach out to that voter and what you say.

That's the dream. The reality is much more chaotic, and the software that does all the tracking isn't perfect. But do your best and don't get caught up in the messiness or imperfection. Whatever list you've got and whatever data you collect will help you make better use of your time than flying completely blind.

PLAN OUT YOUR TIMELINE

Working backward, you'll have to plot out when you talk to which voters about what and how. Start with Election Day and write down your win number—that's your goal.

The final two weeks—and especially four days—before Election Day, make up your get-out-the-vote period (GOTV), which is when all you do is talk about voting. You'll focus on making sure people know when, where, and how to cast their ballot. Everything leading up to those three weeks is about identifying who you'll be talking to in those final weeks. (If there's early voting in your election, adjust your plans accordingly.)

The time between your campaign launch and GOTV is for voter ID. This is campaign shorthand for the work it takes to identify who your possible voters are. Your volunteers can call people and find out what party they're in and who they're planning on voting for. This data will feed back into your voter file and allow you to better winnow down who you focus on as Election Day gets closer.

■ Voter ID also means the various forms of identification a voter might need to bring with them to the polls to prove their identity, depending on how committed the state legislature is to suppressing the vote.

Depending on your timeline, the size of your electorate, and how many volunteers you can get talking on your behalf, you'll be able to do more and talk to more people. You could simultaneously work on voter ID and GOTV messaging; you could add in a team that works explicitly on voter registration or tracking down absentee ballots, or have volunteers who are solely focused on recruiting other volunteers to build that all out.

This is where things get complicated and is why campaigns can become massive organizations with lots of moving pieces—there's tons to keep track of and many competing priorities.

Do NOT get overwhelmed. If you're running a campaign yourself and don't have a huge volunteer network, you can still do this. Just stay focused.

———————

The TL; DR: The best use of your time is talking to voters directly yourself. In the time leading up to Election Day, figure out who those voters are and contact more of them than you need to win. Immediately ahead of Election Day, follow up with everyone you contacted and remind them to vote. Everything else you do is bonus.

Take a deep breath—then figure out your universe.

"Analytics" and "targeting" mean cutting lists of voters to talk to and deciding what to talk to them about. You won't have enough time or money to talk to every single person in your district, so you have to make tough decisions and prioritize.

> ■ Universe: A list of people you're targeting with a specific ask.

Every voter should be measured on two scales:

1: Whether or Not They're Likely to Vote

Voting is a habit. The best indicator that someone's going to vote in the upcoming election is whether or not they voted in the previous elections. Study after study shows that voting in one election increases someone's likelihood of voting in the next election by anywhere from 20 to 50 percentage points.

Analysts quantify this using a "turnout score" on a scale of 1 to 100. Someone with a turnout score of 100 is going to vote, regardless of whether the campaign contacts her or not. Someone with a turnout score of 0 has almost no chance of showing up at the polls.

2: Whether or Not They'll Be Voting for You

The quickest heuristic for determining whether someone will vote for you is their party registration. It's not a perfect indicator, but it's close. If your state doesn't have party registration on the voter file, you might be able to distinguish partisanship based on which primaries that person voted in. If you have data from the state party, you'll know whether they were contacted by previous Democratic campaigns and how they responded.

There are a number of other criteria: demographics, income, consumer data, voting behavior, campaign contact, comparisons to people with similar profiles, polling, and more—that can be factored in to determine how likely a voter is to support you.

Analysts wrap this all up into a "support score"—again, measured on a scale of 1 to 100. One hundred means that the voter is 100 percent likely to support you; 0 means no shot.

In a national or even statewide election with millions and millions of voters, this can quickly get very complicated. Campaigns have to decide what data is relevant in figuring out whether someone is likely to support a candidate—and what's just noise. Analysts will write models and run tests against those models to identify what matters in determining someone's likelihood of supporting—or not supporting—a candidate, and, just as important, what can change that support score. There is a massive industry that's sprung up in the past decade to help campaigns analyze data to figure out the best use of resources (and just as big of a group of people who like to dismiss this "microtargeting" as a waste of resources or as shortsighted).

As with most things, the truth is somewhere in the middle. You're running a small race and you need to make some tough choices about how you spend your time and money, so data is your friend. But don't overthink this. You probably don't have a ton of resources for analytics work, you probably don't know how to build predictive models (I certainly don't!), and you might not be that adept with creating lists in the voter file.

Start simple: Use basic common sense to figure out the people you think will be voting in your election. (Hint: Who voted in the last election similar to yours?) Local elections often have smaller turnout, and the people who show up are habitual voters, especially if the election day isn't part of the usual cycle. Pare that list down to people registered in your party.

That's your base. Someone who votes in every election and always votes for your party might be the first group you reach out to as you build your volunteer team and should definitely be someone you reach out to and ensure they know there's an election.

If the number of people in that universe is bigger than your win number, you're golden. It probably isn't, so keep expanding outward. Add people in your party who regularly voted in the last few elections, and then people in your party who vote sporadically.

■ If you want to dig in on how presidential campaigns use data, pick up a copy of *The Victory Lab* by Sasha Issenberg. It's a great read and the closest thing out there to accurate.

This is not to say you shouldn't go out of your way to find people in the opposing party. But the reality is, if and when you need to prioritize, you should start with the folks likely to be on your side who just need to be nudged to show up at the polls.

There are also certain demographic groups that

are likely to vote for you (if they vote at all). Take that kind of targeting with a grain of salt, but it can be helpful, especially if there's recent polling you can look at to gut-check conventional wisdom.

Ultimately, your campaign should be data-informed but not data-driven-to-the-point-of-ignoring-reality. You should know the numbers, but if your instincts and common sense drive you to a different decision, that's okay. Be able to explain why.

In a small, local race like yours, you likely won't be changing minds as much as helping someone determine their opinion in the first place. Treat the likely voters you'll be talking to as persuasion targets up (people whom you can con-vince to vote for you but who haven't made up their minds yet) until the final GOTV stretch—then treat them like turnout targets (people whom you need to show up at the polls). That doesn't mean your campaign doesn't talk to other voters or even nonvoters, but if you have to decide between two different activities, decide based on which gets you in front of more of those likely voters.

> ■ TL; DR: Get a list of the voters in your district. Figure out which ones are likely to vote for you. Focus your efforts on getting them to the polls.

Make sure you know the different ways people vote.

Knowing how people vote will directly inform your strategy for when to transition from making your case on who to vote for to directly asking them to cast their ballots—for you.

Regulations vary from state to state and even within a single state (and change on a regular basis, because of course they do)—Vote.org is an incredible resource that can help you get started learning the rules where you're running. That being said, there are a few basic categories of when and how people vote.

Absentee Voting/Voting by Mail All states will allow a voter to request and mail in a ballot before Election Day (or bring it in person with them on Election Day) if that voter meets certain criteria—however, those criteria vary dramatically. In some states, the voter needs an excuse, like she'll be out of town, she has a disability, she can't get out of work, or is living overseas. In other states, the elections administrator literally mails every registered voter a ballot, and it's on the voter to return it before or on Election Day.

Early Voting The term "early vote" usually refers to early voting in person before Election Day without having to meet any particular criteria. Most states have some form of early voting; a few have what's called "absentee in-person" voting, where the voter can go into the local election administrator's office and fill out his or her ballot ahead of Election Day. Early voting might begin up to a month before Election Day, or it might only include the seven days before Election Day. It might include Sundays; it might not. Voters might be able to vote early at their usual polling locations; often that's not the case.

Voting on Election Day Exactly what it sounds like. A voter shows up at their polling location, confirms their registration (or, in some states, registers at the polling location), and then casts their ballot. They might have to show ID. They might have to cast what's called a "provisional ballot" if the registration is in question.

■ The rules and regulations around voting are so confusing that it almost seems intentional. That's because it is. Republicans in state legislatures have gone out of their way to set up legal barriers to voting so fewer people will cast their ballots. That's how Republicans believe they win and maintain their seats. Motherfuckers.

As a candidate, you need to be fluent in what a voter in your area needs to know in order to show up to the polls and actually cast a ballot. You should be an expert on the timeline for voter registration and should be able to recite off the top of your head whether a voter needs ID, what kinds of ID satisfy requirements, and whether or not a voter can cast their ballot early. (Or: Know what you don't know and be able to send people to a website to check it out themselves.)

A note on voter registration: For a local campaign, registering voters is really fucking hard—you have to convince people to take the step from never-voted to brand-new-voter-AND-voting-for-you. That is not to say don't do it—but know that your return on investment may be relatively low, so engage with it at your own peril. Reach out to local groups who do year-round voter registration and see what their activity is like in your area. Rock the Vote and the League of Women Voters are two great places to start.

Now pick your tactics.

You have to pick and choose your voter-contact tactics based on the time you've got available, the money you've got to spend, and what works for your community. The best campaign does a mix of multiple approaches coordinated in messaging and timing. Generally speaking, the more personal the tactic, the more likely that tactic is to produce a vote—the smaller and more local the election, the greater impact person-to-person contact has.

In other words: The easier something is to do, the less it probably matters. Sorry.

Tactic No. 1 (and the Way You'll Win): Canvassing

> *"I had numerous doors slammed in my face, and people hung up on me all the time. It can feel defeating at first, but I learned that you have to be resilient and persevere through rejection and keep working hard to earn every vote. You cannot expect that everyone will like you or agree with your policies."*
>
> —CAROLINE SIMMONS, Connecticut state legislator, on her experience canvassing

What it is:
Literally knocking on doors and talking to voters face-to-face. Canvassing (also called door-knocking, block-walking, or hitting the doors) rules.

It is rare to meet a local elected official who doesn't attribute at least one of their wins to their commitment to knocking on doors. Studies show that face-to-face interactions are the most effective method of campaign communication for getting out the vote. Academic political scientists Alan Gerber and Don

Green literally wrote the book on voter communication tactics called *Get Out the Vote*, and they update their studies every couple of years. They even found that one in-person conversation increased turnout by 20 percent. I highly recommend their work.

Dozens of studies over the past two decades have replicated the basic finding that canvassing matters, and it can't just be cursory chatter, either. To actually make a difference, you need to have a real conversation with a voter. You need to meet someone where they're at, learn what they care about, then talk with them about how your goals overlap with their values.

And you have to do it yourself. Yes, you should have volunteers canvass, too—their external validation will go a long way! But at the end of the day, you are the best advocate for your candidacy. Your passion for your community will come through, especially as you get better and better at telling your story with each door you knock on.

> " *I was perpetually surprised by the degree to which people wanted to talk to me when I knocked on their doors. Some people, of course, would tell me, 'I'm busy, come back another time,' but so many people, when they found out I was running for office, had questions and wanted to tell me things. People were, on the whole, excited to have someone show up on their doorstep wanting to talk to them."*
>
> —WILL GUZZARDI, Illinois state legislator, on his experience canvassing

Canvassing is super fun. You can (and should!) bring a friend with you each time you hit the pavement. You and your canvassing pal will get to meet interesting people and will come away with good stories. Every politician worth their salt has a story of canvassing in the snow/rain/[insert crappy weather here], and the fascinating people they met along the way. (It's also good exercise. Seriously. You'll definitely hit and exceed your Fitbit's ten thousand steps every day you canvass.)

Canvassing is the single most important thing you can do to make a difference in the outcome of the election. It's about having real conversations with real people—you'll be surprised at what you learn about what matters. Doing it will make you a better person and, if you win, a better public servant.

Here's how you actually do it:

Start with a list of people to talk to during the canvass. Your voter file will have addresses that you can map with software like NGP VAN or BatchGeo. Pick a street, pick a time, grab a friend, and grab some campaign materials. You'll also want a clipboard and pens to take notes, or, if you're feeling more high-tech, you can use a smartphone or tablet to connect to your voter file online while you walk.

Not to be your overbearing mom, but: If it's hot out, make sure you use sunscreen, sunglasses, and a hat. Put on comfortable walking shoes. If you're driving around, keep an umbrella and raincoat in your car in case the weather changes. And if it's cold and snowy out, have the appropriate gear.

Anyone can canvass on a beautiful springtime day. Winners canvass every day, no matter what the weather is like.

You should always carry literature (also known as "lit") with you. I'll get into different types of campaign lit a little bit later—but for now, just know that it matters to have something to leave behind.

Take your list, find the address, walk up to the door, knock, and, if someone answers, introduce yourself: "Hi! I'm [NAME]. I'm running for [POSITION] here in [TOWN] because [INSERT YOUR REASON FOR RUNNING]. I'd love to talk about what's on your mind. Do you have a few minutes?"

From there, have a little chill. You're probably running in an election that they don't know is even happening, or for a position they've never heard of. That's okay! You'll have to introduce yourself and give a quick biography. You should ask them questions and then actively listen.

President Bill Clinton used to say that he went through life assuming every person could teach him something. Adopt that as your model for canvassing (and also, honestly, for life). Any single person you talk to could spark a thought that could lead to a policy that could make your community better.

Notice the themes you hear over and over again. If folks keep mentioning problems you didn't have as your primary reason for running, ask questions and try to learn more. This kind of listening is literally why you canvass. Don't try and convince someone that your particular passion is more important than the problem they identify—that'll just turn them off. Instead, find common ground where your values and theirs overlap and then work off those shared values to show how you'll solve their problem *and* yours.

Don't get argumentative. Don't try to make a voter feel stupid for not knowing the election is going on. Be a real person, have a real conversation, and, most important, listen. What people really want, more than anything else, is to be heard. They want to know that the things they care about matter to someone else, too. If you aren't sure how to solve the problems they identify, say that, but note that you'll do some research to learn more.

The goal of canvassing is to build a relationship with voters so they remember you, feel invested in you, and show up to vote for you.

Be sure to end every conversation by letting them know when the election is and asking them if they plan on voting. Leave behind your campaign lit so they have something tangible to keep around.

It's important to keep good notes. You want to know how many doors you knocked on in how many hours of canvassing and how many voters you actually talked to. Try to establish a benchmark for this within the first three to five times you canvass. You can better schedule your time to work backward from your win number if you know that, for example, in one hour of canvassing, you're likely to be able to knock on twelve doors and reach four voters.

Make sure you have updated info on the voters you connect with. Anyone you have a conversation with should receive a thank-you note from you within a week, which will remind them that they met with you. (Keep track of that, too!)

Canvass as often as humanly possible. Put it on your calendar and make it sacred time that you can't touch or schedule over. I'm going to say this again: Canvassing is how you win.

There is no app that can canvass for you. There is no shortcut or quick fix to compensate if you don't feel like knocking on doors. But that's a good thing. Consider this: Canvassing is under your control. You can determine your fate if you're willing to put in the work.

A few other tips:

- Wear a name tag or campaign sticker.

- Take off your sunglasses before speaking to someone. That's just polite.

- Don't place anything in a mailbox—that's illegal.

- Don't trample people's flowers. That's not illegal but it's not nice!

- If someone doesn't have time to talk to you, be understanding. Come back later.

Most of the rules for canvassing can be summed up thusly: Show good manners and don't be shitty.

Canvassing is the most important thing you can do as a candidate, and it's the best thing volunteers can do for you, too.

■ **How presidential campaigns do it:** They construct a pyramid scheme of volunteers across the country, with neighborhood team leaders who do "canvass launches" in which they hand out prepped "walk packets" (booklets of maps and scripts) and get volunteers fired up to knock on doors.

■ **How you do it:** You and a friend knock on doors every night after work and every weekend.

"When I began my campaign, I was virtually unknown, I had been living away for over a decade, and I was running against several well-known candidates who were old enough to be my parents. Nobody answered my calls. I was regularly stood up at meetings. My emails were ignored. So I spent my time knocking on doors (lots and lots of doors); showing up to every block party, community picnic, and farmers' market I could find;

and cold-calling hundreds of voters. Eventually that built a buzz, and as Election Day drew closer, all of a sudden those unanswered emails and meeting requests got replies much more quickly."

—ERIC LESSER, Massachusetts state senator, on how he got people to take him seriously

Tactic No. 2: Phone Banks

What it is:

A bunch of people in a room making calls on your campaign's behalf.

What you need:

- Lists of voters for people to call, including phone numbers.

- Scripts: What do you want people to say on the phone? Think about the phase of the campaign you're in. Are your volunteers doing voter ID or GOTV calls? Are you "building for an event" (meaning: inviting people to RSVP for something)? Are you doing follow-up on people you might have met in person when you canvassed or whom you sent mail to? Identify what you're asking people to do and then write out a quick script for volunteers to use.

- A way to collect data: Per usual, if you don't track it, it didn't happen. Ask your volunteers to keep good notes—you could have a regimented spreadsheet where they fill in values based on how the call went.

- Phones. These days, most people are okay using their personal cell phone for this, but you should have a few phones you can hand to people who might not be comfortable with that. Your state party might have phones you can borrow! Ask.

There are a few tools out there (and more launching every day) that let you run a "virtual phone bank." Your campaign can load an app with the call list, the script, and the data-collection mechanism, and then send links to people who want to make calls from home.

This kind of app can be extremely valuable—but it is more work for you to manage and will require troubleshooting. If you have a volunteer serving as your phone bank captain who is also pretty good at using online tools, delegate this task to them.

> ■ **How presidential campaigns do it:** They host in-person phone banks every night of the week in field offices across the country. (Call time is usually 5 to 8 p.m.—when folks are most likely to be home and pick up the phone.) Additionally, they host virtual phone banks online, with coordinated volunteers and teams dedicated to updating lists and scripts, and troubleshooting tech issues.
>
> ■ **How you do it:** Ten people sit around your kitchen table making calls two to three nights a week.

Tactic No. 3: Campaign Literature and Direct Mail

Campaign lit (also called "collateral") has value, even in the age of the internet. Your lit—especially the pieces you directly hand to or mail to voters—will be one of the more tangible and lasting pieces of your campaign. Every voter you talk to should walk away with a piece of lit that can reinforce your message and your name ID.

At the bare minimum, you'll need a palm-size card that you can hand to people. Bigger campaigns with bigger budgets can build out complicated lit programs with more pieces (door hangers, policy plans, booklets, etc.) and GOTV mail that reminds people to vote. If you're expanding past one or two pieces, you should seek out a mail vendor who can help you. Keep in mind they likely get paid based on the number of pieces they send, so take their recommendations with a grain of salt.

> ■ **Name ID:** Literally how many people recognize your name and have an opinion about you. This is something polls measure—and something you influence by getting in front of voters and being memorable.

Your lit has three audiences:

- Three- to four-second scanners who glance at your name and photo before they toss it in the trash.

- Ten- to twenty-second skimmers who will read the headlines and skim the copy.

- Readers who will actually, you know, read it.

You need to appeal to all three. The palm cards that you hand out when you canvass or meet people around town should have your name, your website, your photo, and the day of the election prominently listed.

Mail sent to people's homes (called "direct mail") can be sent widely or be part of a targeted effort, depending on your budget and your resources. You could send mail reinforcing your campaign message, or you could do voter education. If you're looking to send more than one piece of mail, you need to think in terms of a narrative arc and the type of voter you're sending your mail to. You will likely need to send more than one piece of mail to make a difference, because repetition matters. You'll also need to start your mail program earlier than you think—take into account the delay between sending mail and a voter receiving it and actually looking at it.

Know what your goal is for any given mail piece, and don't try to squeeze too much into a single sheet.

To run a complex direct-mail program, you'll likely need to hire a mail consultant, because to do so requires specialized skills like graphic design and voter analysis, and mail-house relationships. You'll probably want to pay someone to handle all that for you.

LEARN MORE ON THE INTERNET Google "political" + "direct mail" + "consultant."

You should take a look at a firm's client lists and their win/loss records. Don't be afraid to ask the party what they recommend. The local staff might have people they work with who know the local scene and are preferred.

When doing budget planning, the biggest expense for direct mail isn't usually design: It's postage. Your state party will have a permit that lets it send mail out at a bulk rate, which can save you money. Your mail, accordingly, might have to have certain disclaimers printed on it—your state party's lawyers can help you navigate this.

If you're running as a Democrat, finding a union printer matters. You've got to walk the walk—support union shops and make sure anything you print has a union bug on it. Union shops are just as affordable and are often used to doing political mail printing.

It's tempting to say mail doesn't matter anymore. (I check my mailbox once a week, and that's only because I get business mail sent to my home.) But most voters aren't like me and probably aren't like you. Especially in smaller local elections, voters are older and more accustomed to getting things via their mailbox. Meet voters where they are and don't play like you're above it.

■ **How presidential campaigns do it:** They hire designers who are dedicated to creating campaign literature in as many languages as needed for the targeted voters, covering every topic and issue imaginable, personalized by state. They run a multitrack direct-mail program that hits targeted voters at a consistent pace, with different budgets and narratives for persuasion, including GOTV or vote-by-mail lit and voter education.

■ **How you do it:** Make a palm card, maybe a door hanger, and if your campaign can afford it, send out one mail piece that tells a little bit about you.

Tactic No. 4: Text Messages

There are two different types of text message programs: Mass texting and one-to-one (or peer-to-peer) texting.

Texting can be used to do anything, from inviting people to events to fundraising to rapidly responding around big moments in your campaign.

■ For whatever reason, in politics, text message programs are still called SMS programs.

Mass texting means using tools like Mobile Commons

113

to send single messages from one organization to a bunch of people. It's technically one-to-many but feels one-to-one, and if done right, can be very expensive to run. Building a list can be hard—each person legally has to opt in to receiving mass text messages from your campaign, and the law is strict on this—and the voter file doesn't usually have cell phone numbers on it. Many vendors will make you pay by message sent, so you need to plan carefully.

Another option is to run a peer-to-peer texting program, in which an organizer or volunteer sends text messages to voters individually. Because it's not technically a "blast" text message, people don't have to opt in—basically, you're sending text messages to strangers who didn't ask for them. It's not as easy, necessarily, but it's often cheaper.

Regardless of which type of SMS program you choose (or if you decide to do both; they're not mutually exclusive), it'll likely move the needle.

Outside of canvassing and phone calls, texting is one of the few scientifically proven ways to increase turnout; some studies in 2010 found text messages increased turnout by as much as 3 percent, in part because they're personal, targeted, and hard to ignore. (Only a monster is okay with seeing unread text message notifications on their phone.) Text messages tend to reach communities that are often harder to communicate with through more old-fashioned voter contact channels: Young people, communities of color, and folks who move a lot respond well to text messages.

The downside is that running a text message program well can be expensive and requires specialized skills.

If you're interested, start by scoping out the landscape.

LEARN MORE ON THE INTERNET Google "political campaign" + "text messages." You might see some tools pop up, like Hustle, Mobile Commons, Twilio, and many others. That means you're on the right track.

> ■ **How presidential campaigns do it:** They spend years building up an SMS list and run targeted programs for fundraising, mobilization, and supporter engagement over mass text. They use peer-to-peer text messages to encourage voters to return their ballots, confirm RSVPs for events, and recruit volunteers.
>
> ■ **How you do it:** You probably don't, unless you can afford it or have the staff and volunteers to help manage and execute on it. But you should look into it, because it can be valuable!

Tactic No. 5: Visibility (or "viz")

This is just people standing on street corners with posters or rally signs. It definitely doesn't matter for voter contact. But it'll make people feel good, and if you need to do something to show momentum or enthusiasm around your campaign for press optics, this will do the trick.

> ■ **How presidential campaigns do it:** Before every big event, they recruit supporters to do viz to show the press that there's enthusiasm. They get people jumping, holding signs, and wearing T-shirts.
>
> ■ **How you do it:** If you have folks who are eager to stand outside with signs and show enthusiasm, great! Otherwise, don't ask people to do this. You can use their time in better ways.

Tactic No. 6: Robocalls

Ever picked up the phone and heard an automated recording of a voice start talking to you? That's a robocall. They are a relatively cheap way to contact voters. They also make little to no impact on turnout. In the final weeks, campaigns often run out of ways to spend money (you can't place any additional ads after a certain date; you can't pay for more canvassers, etc.), so if you have money to spend, robocalls certainly can't hurt. Make sure to check state law, because in some places they might be illegal.

Tactic No. 7: The Internet

You have to be on social media. This is not optional. You don't need to be everywhere, but you do need to be on Twitter and Facebook. (If you're buying this book, you're probably already on these platforms—if you're not, fix that.)

There are dozens of social media platforms you could decide to join, and new ones popping up every month. Focus your efforts on the ones where you can reach either journalists or voters. Any social media account will require maintenance, so pick the ones you're on organically and fit that with who you are.

Before you launch your campaign, apply a critical eye to all of your public profiles. Adjust your privacy settings on anything you don't want people to immediately consider one of your campaign accounts. Delete any photos and posts that might get you into trouble, but don't take this too seriously or panic too much. Know what's out there but don't overthink it. Then focus in on the accounts you'll keep updating as part of your campaign.

Twitter Twitter is for reaching two key groups: journalists and activists. Most voters aren't hanging out on Twitter all day, reading political Twitter (or any other subset of Twitter, for that matter, like sports Twitter or ShondaLand Twitter). Journalists, however, use Twitter as a way to share stories, talk with other journalists, and hear about breaking news as soon as it happens. If you want to get in front of reporters, start by following them on Twitter and engaging with their tweets.

Activists on Twitter tend to talk around particular hashtags. Once you've identified the political leaders in your community, find them on Twitter. Look at who they follow and who follows them. You'll start to see some common figures—the people who pop up regularly and who have vibrant Twitter presences are who you should aim to connect with. Follow them, reply to them, and retweet them.

Your goal on Twitter is not to reach as many people as possible but to reach the right people and make it seem like "everyone" is talking about you and your campaign. This will give the impression that your campaign is newsworthy, which will get you press, which will then help you get in front of even more voters and reinforce your name recognition.

Your social media presence on Twitter should be true to you. Think of the politicians you like best on Twitter: You could probably sum up their "brand" in a few big words. They usually tweet about a mix of political topics, issues, and their personal interests (sports, cooking, theater, their kids, etc.) Pick your lanes and stick with them. Be you! Show pictures from the trail, talk about people you meet, share news stories you find interesting, retweet people talking about your campaign, and don't be afraid to engage with the haters.

Facebook Facebook is about reaching real people. At this point, it is not an exaggeration to say that nearly everyone is on Facebook.

You can create a Facebook page based on your profile—just search the Facebook help section. The "page" format will give you audience insights, allow you to run advertising, and keep your "personal" profile separate from your public persona.

Think strategically about your cover image, your profile photo, your "about" section, and all the little details (like your timeline and the other things your page "likes"). Make sure it's coherent.

Post regularly and give people on-message #content to like and share. The more people immediately engage with something, the more newsfeeds it'll pop up in, thus giving more people a chance to engage

■ A rule of thumb for all social media platforms, now that you're a candidate for office: Be a real person. (It helps that you *are* a real person. . . .) Always assume that anything you post, share, like, or promote could land on the front page of your local newspaper, and act accordingly. Also: Proofread yourself. Typos are just embarrassing.

with it. The algorithm is a motherfucker, but you'll be able to see the analytics on your posts to know what works and what doesn't.

People share things or like things in order to (subconsciously) curate a particular image of themselves. Think critically about how you and your friends use Facebook, what you share, and what you see your parents and grandparents sharing. Perhaps you share something because you want to be associated with the story or the values it represents, or because you want to explicitly comment as being *not* a part of something. Look at your newsfeed and ask yourself what reasons people might have for sharing, liking, or posting something.

One thing Facebook is great for: live video. You can live-stream any event on Facebook through your smartphone and reach your fans and your fans' friends. Be creative about this! Driving through your town and feel like live-streaming your trip? Do it. Want to live-stream your town hall? Yes, please.

Use Facebook as a tool to further your campaign's goals. You're not bugging people; anyone who likes your page will want to see what you're providing to them.

Instagram Instagram can be fun for sharing photos from the trail. It's not necessarily worth a huge investment of your time if you're not already on Instagram, but if it's part of your daily routine already, keep on using it and just be intentional about what you share.

Other Social Media Platforms If writing comes easy to you, blogging can be a great way to get your thoughts out in a shareable platform. Try Medium or Tumblr, or something like WordPress. Again, don't devote too much time to this if you're not comfortable with it.

You should set up a YouTube channel for your campaign, and if you happen to make commercials, you should post them on YouTube so people can embed and share them. If there are TV newsclips about you, post those as well.

If your campaign gets big and you end up with a lot of photos you want to disseminate, creating a public Flickr account or joining a similar kind of photo-sharing service that lets you create captions and offers licensing will give people a way to find them easily. This is lower on the priority list.

Email Email is a direct line to your supporters in a way that is both personal and targeted. It's the best. I should admit my bias here: I got my start in politics writing and sending fundraising emails. I love it so much. It's a special mix of creativity and science, and the impact is immediate: Ask people to do something that matters and then they do it! It's addictive. I will always hold a special place in my heart for email marketing.

But my biases aside, email is the cockroach of the internet—no matter how many apps pop up or how many other platforms shake out, people will still have email addresses and still use email as one of their primary communication channels. And for your campaign, email will be one of the main ways you raise money online. I'll dig more into that in the next section, on fundraising.

You should prioritize building an email list and you should send emails to everyone on it. Again, don't be afraid of bothering people. (No matter how many emails you send, you won't come close to matching the volume of some of the committees or a presidential campaign.) People who sign up to join your list are supporters. They don't need convincing that your race matters—they're already on board. They just need to be told what to do to help you and when to do it. You can ask people on your email list to donate (and you should!), but you should also ask your supporters to volunteer, to attend events, to ask their friends to sign up, to share videos or articles, and to vote!

When writing email, be quick, be authentic, and ask people to do exactly what you want them to (and don't apologize for it). Make it easy for people to do what you ask of them.

There are a few tools you can use to send email.

LEARN MORE ON THE INTERNET Google "political campaign" + "email service provider."

You might want to use MailChimp or something like Constant Contact. If you're a Democrat, you could also use Action Network or Salsa, and if you've got more money and technologically savvy friends, you could scope out Blue State

Digital. NGP VAN, which is the official Democratic tool for donation intake and compliance reasons, also has an email tool. Again, ask your state party what they recommend.

Website You do need a website. If you're running in the twenty-first century and you don't have an online presence, it's almost as if you don't exist. That's not hyperbolic: If a voter can't Google you and find some proof of your campaign quickly and easily, they'll assume you're a scam.

Search engine optimization (SEO) is important. When building your website, make sure your metadata has your name and relevant key words embedded. While writing your headlines and text, consider what people might search in order to find you. Unfortunately, there isn't much you can do to game the Google algorithm beyond buying paid ads.

Your website does *not* need to be complicated. Go online right now and claim your domain name. Keep it simple (think: yourfullname.com, voteyourfullname .com, or something along those lines). If you think you might run for another position one day, don't put the current position or year in the URL. If you can't avoid that, do it. Honestly, it doesn't really matter. Just make it something easy to remember—your URL will be going on all of your campaign materials.

Look for a self-service site builder—anything with clean templates that's easy to use and cheap, and has integrations with other online services that will make your campaign easier to run.

You'll need a simple logo. It could be as lo-fi as your name in a standout font. Forget everything you've seen for presidential campaigns or even congressional races. For a local race like yours, keep it extremely simple. Ask your friends and family for help; if someone is a professional graphic designer willing to do this for free, great. If not, there are a few tools online you can find that'll help you make a logo. Do *not* get caught up in the details like this; just pick something you like and stick with it.

Your website should be clean and easy to read, and should offer everything people expect out of a campaign website:

- A voter might seek out your site to find out more about you. Accordingly, your website should have a biography of you, and photos.

- They might want to give you money. We'll talk more about fundraising on page 141—but for now, just know: Your website should have a donate function front and center.

- People will likely want to get involved with your campaign. You should have a way for them to sign up for your campaign emails and, more explicitly, to volunteer—and that information should feed into a system that someone checks and follows up on. Some tools will spit out a Google sheet for you, or could integrate into other services.

Your website should also include information on how to contact you and your campaign. Set up a campaign email address (info@your-url-here.com or hello@your-url-here.com) as well as one for press (press@your-url-here.com) and give those out to anyone who asks. Be sure those inboxes get checked; get volunteers who will help keep an eye on them (especially the press inbox!).

You don't need to have a site that has a regularly updated blog—you can post longer-form notes on Medium or even Facebook. You don't even need to list all your policy positions on your website—you could just have links to posts on a freestanding site. In all likelihood, you'll be running against someone who's less comfortable using the internet as a tool for communication. Take advantage of that and get your stuff out there as much as possible.

> ■ **How presidential campaigns do it:** They hire teams of two-hundred–plus people to run multiple accounts, build out tech tools, and manage online communities. They invest hundreds of millions of dollars. The teams innovate, test, and have nearly every resource at their disposal.

> ■ How you do it: Got an internet-savvy friend? Ask them to take the lead. These accounts all take time to manage, and it might not be the best use of your time as a candidate to be tweeting and posting on Facebook all day. Pick a friend who knows you pretty well and could mimic your voice. Set out clear goals for your social platforms and make sure they know what you'd want to okay yourself before they post and what you'd be okay with them YOLO'ing. Pick the platforms where your people are and focus there.

Tactic No. 8: Yard Signs

Yard signs don't vote. But they do often remind people there's an election. Your union printer who does your mail and lit can help you get yard signs.

> ■ How presidential campaigns do it: They use yard signs as a way to get volunteers in the door (as in: Come pick up your yard sign at the local field office!) and then sign people up.
>
> ■ How you do it: Your campaign gets marginally more of a benefit from a yard sign than a presidential campaign does, since you probably don't have 90 percent name recognition in your community. Offer yard signs to volunteers for free if they complete a phone bank or volunteer shift.

Tactic No. 9: Paid Media (or, Advertising)

Every campaign should run digital advertising. People spend, on average, nearly an hour a day on Facebook. (That's probably an understatement.) Nearly 80 percent of the United States is on the platform, so meet people where they're at. You can run targeted ads on Facebook to people directly in your community through your page and get a pretty good cost per impression. You can run click-to-website ads to get people joining your email list, to push a policy platform, or to let people learn more about your bio. Any paid ads you run on Facebook will also grow your organic following because more people will like your page—but because Facebook is incentivized to make you spend money, you're going to have to pay to really reach a substantial number of people.

If you're going to run video ads on Facebook (and you should if you have the content!), make sure they're short and that they have closed captions.

Facebook will let you target your audience both geographically and by interest. If it makes sense, you can restrict your ads to people who identify as Democrats (or progressives or liberals, or people who like Barack Obama and similar Democratic figures). Don't read the comments on your ads.

On Google, you can pay to use a service called AdWords to show up at the top of the first page of search results for any given key word. You only pay per click, and you can geo-target prospective voters to ensure your ads are showing up only for people in your state or city.

Google AdWords will also let you run video as "pre-roll" in YouTube videos—and as of writing, Google will only charge you for a completed watch. Consider recording a bio video on your iPhone, then running it on YouTube. You'll likely be one of the few local candidates trying this.

> ■ Nearly 90 percent of Facebook users watch videos on their phones, which means the volume is often muted. Make sure your ad is effective without sound.

If you want to take it to the next level, you can run e-commerce-style ads online to reach your voters multiple times. You could go so far as to do retargeting (meaning showing ads to people after they've visited your website, through cookie-tracking) and even voter file matching (where you upload your voter target list to Facebook, see what you can match, based on email addresses, and then show ads explicitly to those voters). If you have the money and tech-savviness to do it, you could follow people around on the internet. If you don't have the money or tech to do this, don't fret. It's all icing on the cake.

The best thing about online ads is that you can test them and see what the response rate is. If one ad on Facebook gets extraordinarily high engagement and another doesn't, you can get immediate feedback on whether a message resonates.

For all of this, there are firms that can help you if you want to go big. You'll want to assess what other clients they have, what kind of program they'll want to run (meaning: list-building, persuasion, or mobilization) and what they'll cost. Some firms charge a retainer fee plus a commission on ad spend; others just do the commission on what you spend. Consider the fact that any consultant you bring on, you'll have to manage, or have someone on your team manage.

LEARN MORE ON THE INTERNET Google "political campaign" + "digital advertising" + "consultant."

It might also make sense to run ads on the radio, depending on the demographic you're hoping to reach. Rural populations, African Americans, and Latinos turn to local radio as part of their community's communication channels. If you have the budget and the stations in your area to reach your target voters, you could layer radio ads in as another part of your campaign's communication. This is another area where you might want a consultant to help you out.

LEARN MORE ON THE INTERNET Google "political campaign" + "radio advertising" + "consultant" + "[YOUR STATE]."

Depending on the size of your campaign, you're probably only spending money on digital ads and maybe radio ads. Unfortunately, print newspaper ads aren't really a thing anymore, outside of digital ads purchased on newspaper websites, and TV ads probably don't make sense for your campaign. Depending on the media market, you probably can't afford it.

■ Media market: The region reached by a TV or radio station. For example: The DC media market actually includes people who live as far away as Baltimore or the outer suburbs in Virginia. Ads there cost a *lot* of money.

You might be tempted to run TV ads, but remember that TV is a pay-and-spray medium, for lack of a better phrase. You'll pay a lot and likely get in front of a whole lot of people who are not your voters. For presidential campaigns, ad buyers will target cable networks and can often do house-by-house targeting to show people in the same neighborhood different ads. Your campaign can't afford that and, given the size of your race, shouldn't waste the money on it.

Tactic No. 10: Earned Media (or, the Press)

"Earned media" is a jargony way of saying "getting reporters to pay attention to you."

How to get reporters to give a shit in three easy steps:

Be newsworthy. Yes, it is that simple. You need to be newsworthy, meaning you need to generate clicks or eyeballs (or retweets) for an outlet. You need to either be novel, controversial, or interesting.

Be timely. As a local candidate, you probably can't set the narrative, but you can attach yourself to what's going on and find a way to make it relevant to your voters.

Make friends with local reporters. Once again, your relationships are your greatest currency. Build out a press list by scouring Twitter and news websites for the email addresses of the press who cover your race as part of their beat—you can also ask your state or local party if they have a press list they work off of. Find the local city desk reporter, or the local politics reporter, or if you're running for school board, the education reporter. Include local radio stations, bloggers, TV producers, and anyone else who has a platform that reaches voters. You'll be tempted to add national press (like the *New York Times* or *USA Today*). Don't. Big national outlets might seem "sexy" but your local outlets will ensure your message is getting in front of your voters.

Once you launch, send each of those folks an individual email offering to introduce yourself and get a cup of coffee. Over coffee, establish yourself as speaking "off the record," then have a real human conversation! Mention stories they've written recently that you've read. Ask what would make their job easier. Find out what specifically they find interesting and then, after the meeting is over, take notes so you don't forget.

Everything you do can be earned media. Put out a fun video? Email it to the reporters you had coffee with to make sure they see it. If even one tweets it, great! Retweet that reporter on your campaign account and create a feedback loop. Get an endorsement? Send out a press release to your press list and offer to connect them with the endorser.

Don't be a pain in the ass—reporters are real people. Don't inundate them with formulaic letters to the editor, don't pick unnecessary fights with them, and don't antagonize them in public. It works for Trump but it won't work for you. Don't ever lie. You'll lose your credibility. Say you don't know, or say you'll look into it, but treat your relationship with the press as carefully as you treat any voter you meet while canvassing.

> ■ Yes, Republicans lie all the fucking time. It's infuriating! But Republicans have a base that's inclined not to believe the press anyway. A fact checker who gives a GOPer an F doesn't really get hurt, because GOP voters don't trust the fact checker to begin with. You're better than that. Don't lie.

Reporters have deadlines they have to meet and bosses they have to satisfy. Send out press releases when they're relevant or interesting, but don't flood a reporter's inbox. If you become known as a spammer, when you have something you really want to get their attention with, folks will be used to ignoring you.

Finally, assume best intentions, but know that everyone makes mistakes. Most reporters aren't out to screw you. They're real people with tough jobs and they're under a lot of scrutiny. Make their lives a little easier and your campaign will go far in the media. At the same time, keep in mind that reporters are not perfect. Remember that anything you say or send to them could eventually find its way into the public eye, so think carefully.

You can get media training if you're really nervous or just want to brush up on your skills. Candidate-training programs often include this; otherwise, you can reach out to a political communications consulting firm and ask if they offer one-off media trainings for local candidates. A warning: These services can often be expensive.

LEARN MORE ON THE INTERNET Google "political campaign" + "media training" + "[YOUR STATE]."

A tip for talking to reporters: Before an interview, know what you want the headline of the story to be. It's okay not to explicitly answer a question; just quickly pivot to what you want to say in order to get to that headline. Practice, practice, practice. Ask friends to pepper you with questions and see if you can stay on message and focused. If you're going on TV, record yourself with a camera, then put your discomfort aside and watch the tape.

> ■ David Axelrod, chief advisor to Barack Obama, once quotably said: "Campaigns are like an MRI for the soul—whoever you are, eventually people find out." Know ahead of time what that MRI will reveal.

Tactic No. 11: Surrogates and Endorsements (or, Other People)

Endorsements matter in a local race: When voters don't know much about you as a person, they'll measure you in at least some part by whether or not a known entity has endorsed you. If you're endorsed by, say, Planned Parenthood or NARAL Pro-Choice America, voters know what that means about your values.

Groups that endorse tend to raise your profile by sending out a press release, a statement, email, or post on social media about you, helping you to reach their audiences. Some endorsements come with money or volunteer support. You could also be invited to events put on by the endorsing organization where you can meet individuals who could help your campaign.

Organizations that endorse candidates often have questionnaires you have to fill out. You might have to sit for an interview.

> ■ Sad but true: People are a little bit lazy. Think about how you go about life—how do you know what books to read? What movies to see? What restaurants to try? You look to reviews from critics, or recommendations from friends. Voters do the same when deciding between candidates: They look to others with good judgment to do the screening and tell them what's what.

Treat those questionnaires and interviews as communications that might one day be public.

Personal endorsements matter, too, depending on the person. When you did your political lay-of-the-land research, you probably identified a few of the big names in your community. Maybe it's a small-business owner, maybe it's a local celebrity, maybe it's just a guy in town who knows everyone and everything and is a "tastemaker" in your community. This person's endorsement will influence others. Individuals who endorse and then advocate on your behalf are called "surrogates."

Surrogates can help with fundraising and press—and, depending on the person's network, they can act as an advocate for you with their friends, who can then write checks. If the surrogate is newsworthy, you can ask them to talk to reporters on your behalf.

■ How presidential campaigns do it: One example: Bruce Springsteen plays a concert in North Carolina where organizers do data collection at the door; afterward, everyone goes to vote early. The media covers it, the campaign makes videos of it, and voters who might not have shown up for a political speech or cared about the candidate otherwise (but fucking love Bruce) get engaged.

■ How you do it: You connect with local elected officials, court them, and convince them to publicly support you. You send their statements out to press, you send them in front of donors, and you ask them to tweet or post on Facebook about you. Then you share their posts. You also retweet or share real people who talk about you online, in order to demonstrate that others are supporting your campaign.

7

MESSAGE
(OR, WHAT YOU TALK TO VOTERS ABOUT)

■ **The tactics and channels you use** to reach voters matter; just as important is what you say once you have voters' attention.

TL; DR: Be you. Be chill. Don't be an asshole. Don't lie.

DEVELOPING YOUR CAMPAIGN MESSAGE

The key thing to remember is that voters don't really give a shit about you. (Sorry!) What voters care about is how you will help them. You're asking something big of a voter: You're asking them to let you make decisions that will directly impact their lives. Representative democracy means they're delegating the governing to you and they're trusting you to behave with their best interests at heart. They're electing you to get informed and do the work so they don't have to.

You'll need to give voters a compelling reason to give you that responsibility. A voter needs to like you, trust you, believe you, and be informed on where you stand and how you make decisions. Your campaign message needs to connect your story to their lives in a clear and straightforward way. It needs to be comprehensible in ten seconds, thirty seconds, one minute, five minutes, ten minutes, and a half hour. You need to be able to say it simply and passionately, and you need to believe it enough to repeat it over and over again without getting bored with yourself.

Go back to that original reason why you're running for office—the problem you want to solve and how the office you're running for lets you solve it. Then take a step back: What are the values behind that problem? Why does it upset you, or why do you want to improve upon it?

For example: You're running for city council because you are frustrated that your town doesn't offer solar power as an option on electricity bills. Why do you really care about this? Is it because of a passion for fighting climate change to protect the future of the planet? Or is it because you want electricity bills to be cheaper because families deserve to keep more of their paychecks? Could be both, could be neither, could be something else entirely.

Defining your campaign message requires some introspection. You've got to ask yourself key questions, like:

- Why am I doing this?

- Why should people trust me?

- What are my strengths as a leader?

- What are my weaknesses?

- What do I care about? And, just as importantly: What do I not care about?

- What parts of my life and my story am I most proud of?

- What am I ashamed of? What do I hope people will never find out?

- Why do I want to win this election? More important: Why should a voter want me to win this election?

If you'll notice, developing a campaign message is a lot like being an angsty teenager going through therapy. That's the point! Your campaign is selling a product—YOU!—and you need to know that product inside and out, and be comfortable with the product's selling points.

Develop a campaign theme—the rationale for why you're running. On a very basic level, if you're a challenger, you're usually arguing for change. Incumbents tend to argue for continuity—more of the same. Slogans are helpful in that they sum up your campaign argument in a pithy way, but don't overthink it. What you're trying to make sure people remember is your name and that there's an election happening on a specific day. Anything else is bonus.

Remember: You're not just competing against your opponent in the election. You're also competing against everything else—other news, errands, family obligations, dogs that need walking, tweets that need sharing, and friends that need celebrating. Your story needs to break through, so once you've got a voter's attention, don't waste it.

DRAW THE CLASSIC MESSAGE BOX

WHAT YOU SAY ABOUT YOURSELF	WHAT THEY SAY ABOUT THEMSELVES
WHAT YOU SAY ABOUT YOUR OPPONENT	WHAT YOUR OPPONENT SAYS ABOUT YOU

You should do one of these message boxes for your campaign as a whole and then one for each issue, and one for each of your opponents. It's valuable for thinking through how you're going to talk about your opponent and how you're going to defend yourself when your opponent talks about you.

This message box isn't a stagnant thought-exercise. Do it and ask your team to do it, too—make sure you're all on the same page on how you're conceptualizing your campaign message.

You're winning when the campaign narrative is on your terms—when you're working from the top-left box. You're losing when the campaign is on your opponent's terms, in the lower right-hand box.

TESTING YOUR MESSAGING THROUGH POLLING AND FOCUS GROUPS

Presidential campaigns can run massive polling operations, do daily tracking, run modeling, and hold regular focus groups to identify what messaging resonates with voters. You probably won't have the money or, honestly, the sample size to do this, nor will you likely have the name recognition to make it worth doing.

Test where you can—try different ways of explaining the same point on social media and see which post does best. Notice when you're speaking in front of groups what argument gets people's heads nodding and what gets them tuning out and checking their phones. Trust the reaction you get from voters when you're canvassing or talking to people at events, and then adjust accordingly. If you keep getting the same questions over and over again, try to preempt them.

WRITING YOUR STUMP SPEECH

Your stump speech is the spiel you'll give every single day at every single event. It should include your bio, your vision for the community, your ties back to your community, and a compelling case for why someone should vote for you. End it with a call to action—maybe asking the crowd to join your campaign, or maybe asking folks to volunteer—and articulate a specific way to do that, like going to your website or finding an organizer. You should have a short stump speech, a longer version, and the longest version. The speech should be second nature to you.

When writing your stump speech, write or talk like a real person. Don't pretend to be a politician; you're not a politician and that's part of your selling point. You can and should use language that comes naturally.

Use fewer words per square thought. Concision is valuable. (There's a reason Twitter is a prominent platform for communication: You're forced to be concise in 140 characters or less.)

Be consistent. You might get tired of telling the same stories or using the same talking points over and over again, but the voters you're talking to will be hearing them for the first time, nearly every time. Repetition will help your message stick. No one is going to say, "Ugh, this lady keeps repeating herself," because, sadly, few people are paying attention enough to hear it more than once.

Public speaking might be a little scary— but you can do this.

Public speaking for your campaign is different from the usual speech you might be afraid of giving. You're not talking about something abstract or something you have to do research into. You're talking about you, your passion for the community, and the problem you want to solve. This isn't rocket science (unless space exploration is part of your platform). It's you and what you care about. You're running because you're passionate about doing something good for your neighbors, and if you can channel that when you speak, you'll be successful.

A few suggestions . . .

- Read the room. A good public speaker meets the crowd where they're at, then takes them on an emotional ride using variations in tone, volume, and cadence. Are folks hyped? Start out hyped too! Is the audience sleepy? Acknowledge it, speak slowly and at a low volume, then build up to being energized.

- Make sure your body language matches what you're actually saying. Most communication is nonverbal. Stand up straight, make eye contact with the crowd, and don't be afraid of speaking with your hands, if that's what you normally do.

- It's okay to be nervous! You'll get better with practice. Do some low-stakes speaking before it's too much pressure. (I find smaller crowds of people I know to be more stressful than big groups of strangers—but that's just me.)

Do self-research—and don't get taken by surprise.

You need to know what's out there about you. Start with public records: Have you ever been arrested or dealt with the court system? That kind of information will be available for someone to dig up. Google yourself and see what's easily accessible in the first three to five pages of results. Find the pictures and videos that are online, and take a look at your social media accounts. Make sure you've paid your taxes, especially the local ones. (Nothing's worse than someone arguing for the ability to raise or lower taxes but doesn't bother to pay his or her own.)

If you know about it and own it, you can handle it. Don't run from your past or what's out there on you. Turn it into part of your story. You dealt with some shit and came out a better person. Also, as we've discussed before, who among us hasn't made some mistakes? You probably didn't get caught on tape bragging about sexually assaulting women, so you're fine.

Make sure your team knows all the dirt on you. If you declared bankruptcy once, or were arrested for something in your past, that's all okay. But your inner circle should know these things and should never get caught unawares if they come up during the campaign.

Looks matter. (Sorry.)

You know the old expression "Dress for the job you want, not the job you have"?

That's true for campaigns. Dress like a professional. Athleisure might be comfy but it's probably not going to endear you to too many voters.

Women, this is where the patriarchy really fucks us over. What is the right amount of cleavage to show? How short of a skirt is too short? Can you ever wear shorts? Should you wear lipstick? What does it say about you if you wear your hair natural?

The answer is up to you: You know what your community will deem "acceptable" and what it won't. The shitty truth of being a woman in politics (and in life) is that nothing you do will satisfy everyone, so go with what you're comfortable with and what you feel accurately represents your personality and presentation. Most women in politics wear pantsuits for a reason: They look professional without distracting from the message the woman wants to get across.

If you're canvassing, don't wear high heels or be overdressed. Suits probably aren't necessary for men. Keep the weather in mind and wear lighter colors and looser fabrics; you don't want pit stains when you're trying to introduce yourself to voters.

> ■ Being a politician in the twenty-first century means keeping Photoshop in mind. Never pose for a picture while holding up a white piece of paper; someone could electronically manipulate it into something else entirely. Some politicians have a rule about never wearing anything on their heads.

The golden rule: Don't lie to people.

> " *People know each other! You've got to be careful. You might have a political opponent who you're tempted to let have it, but then you realize their kids are friends with yours, maybe, or you're going to run into that person's mother at the grocery store. It really makes you think.*"
>
> —PETE BUTTIGIEG, mayor of South Bend, IN, on keeping it classy

It's easy to say that in the era of Trump, facts don't matter. Don't take the low road on this: Truth is important, and you should hold yourself to a higher standard than President Grabby Hands. When you don't have an answer to someone's question, say so! Be honest and tell people, "Thank you for bringing that up—I don't know enough yet. Where do you stand?" Turn it around on the voter and then genuinely listen!

Voters won't forgive your bullshitting them. If they're asking about something, it's something they know a lot about and they'll smell your crap a mile away. They have an emotional investment in your answer, so don't turn them against you.

If you do your research on your district and really know the lay of the land, you'll be prepared for the big questions that might come up.

HOW TO LEARN ALL THE THINGS YOU'LL NEED TO KNOW

No one can feed you the answers. Your party can help you figure out the bare bones of where you might consider standing on the issues, but you've got to do the research. If you're clearly uninformed, it'll show. Reach out to advocacy groups in your community and ask for their research books. Set up meetings and ask them to come and teach you.

Doing this research might help you discover passions you didn't know you had. Maybe you got into the race because you care about a woman's right to choose—and in researching the issues relevant to your opponent, you discovered he or she had an abhorrent record on transportation funding, which explains why you were sitting in traffic every day because the construction crews were underfunded. You never know what you might learn!

> ■ Psychology hack: Asking people for help or advice makes them more inclined to like you. You're showing vulnerability and flattering them for their expertise. Don't play stupid, but if it makes sense, consider asking someone to explain something, both to learn and to strengthen your relationship with him or her.

HOW TO HANDLE DEBATES

Debates are the fucking best—for both the participant and the engaged citizen.

As a candidate, especially if you're challenging an incumbent, you should ask for a debate—and you should seriously consider agreeing to participate in any debate or forum offered to you. You get a chance to talk through the differences between you and your opponent, hold your opponent accountable for their stances, and get some earned media out of it. And if you say yes but your opponent declines to participate, you get a chance to ask what he or she is hiding—always a fun argument to make.

That being said, debates aren't for everyone. Maybe you're not as quick on your feet, or you're feeling confident that your campaign is on the right track and you don't need to spend two hours in a community center room opening yourself up to an unforced error. If you're not 100 percent sure a debate will help your campaign, it's okay to decline. (Most voters won't know or care.)

If you decide to move forward with the event, make sure you or a representative of your campaign negotiates the logistics. You can argue over details big and small, including: debate format, speaking order, length of remarks, moderators, audience members, topics, location, date, press distribution, whether or not there are podiums, what is permitted onstage, and literally anything else under the sun.

Once you've confirmed the debate is happening, you have to prepare. Political debates are unlike any other kind of debate. You're not actually trying to argue with anyone. Instead, you're trying to make a point, pivot to your position, and punch back at your opponent.

Set aside some time in your schedule leading up to the debate to work on what you want to say and how you want to say it. Have your communications director or a few smart friends form a "debate prep team" and pull together a list of possible questions that might come up, then work up answers. Great one-liners don't usually happen organically the night-of—they're prepared ahead of time and practiced until they seem natural.

The prep team should also think strategically about what your opponent might say, both in response to questions from the moderator and in response to your arguments. All of this prep needs to keep in mind the debate rules, including time limitations and any parameters around opening statements and closing remarks.

After you've had time to review the prep materials, do at least one mock debate. Find someone to play your opponent and ask him or her to study up on your opponent's argumentative style and likely responses. Have another person play the moderator, set up cameras in the back, and go forth with your debate. Review the tape after to see where you struggled. Don't just think about what you say; keep in mind how you look when you say it. Do you fidget? Are your eyes glancing around the room? Do you speak with your hands? Be aware of how you present yourself.

On the night of the debate, keep three things in mind: Speak slowly, stay on message, and claim victory. It matters less what happens onstage (or at the community center common room) and more about what you say and how you posture yourself afterward. You won! Shout it from the rooftops (or tweet it a lot, and have supporters and surrogates do the same). If the debate is televised or live-streamed, make sure your supporters and validators know about it and tune in. Have someone on your team ready to arm them with guidance on how to talk about the debate afterwards, whether it's via email or a conference call shortly after the event ends.

Debates are a chance for voters to compare you and your opponent head to head. Relax, have fun, and congratulations on your debate victory.

WHEN YOU GET TO GOTV: DO'S AND DON'TS WHEN TALKING ABOUT VOTING

Repeat after me: Voting is quick, easy, and everyone is doing it. Consider getting that tattooed on your arm. Voting is quick! It's easy! Everyone is doing it! Anything counter to that message could dissuade someone from voting. More specifically . . .

DO

- Play up that it's their civic duty to vote.

- Ask people if they have a plan for voting. Just the act of thinking about the logistics of voting can lead to someone actually casting their ballot.

- Remind folks that voting records are public (but who they vote for is private) Do this in a non-creepy way. It's probably best communicated through mail or campaign literature (or online).

DO NOT

- Mention lines. Who wants to wait in a line? No one. Lines suck.

- Tell someone their vote will matter more because of low turnout. Even if that's true, that's not why people vote. They vote because their friends are doing it, and they'll feel embarrassed if they're the only one who didn't vote. That's why you get a sticker when you vote: It's public proof you did your civic duty.

- Promise anything (like money or a gift) in exchange for a vote. That's a legal no-no.

8

MONEY
(OR, HOW TO RAISE
WHAT YOU NEED)

■ **One of the biggest reasons** people decide not to run is because of the money. I get it. Raising money seems scary.

But it's important. Do not ever be embarrassed or ashamed to ask someone to contribute to your campaign, and don't apologize for doing so, either. You're not asking someone to loan you money for lunch. You're asking someone to invest in their values and do something good for their community. If you're running a fiscally responsible race and spending your resources on voter contact, you're not scamming anyone. In fact, you could even think of it as doing someone a public service: You're giving people a way to actually do something with their beliefs. You're providing them a way to get involved.

Say what you believe and stand by your positions. The people who want to invest in your race will give to you. Those who don't agree with you, won't.

WHY YOU HAVE TO RAISE MONEY

Well, for one thing, you have to pay for stuff. Don't pull a Trump and stiff your vendors or contractors for labor.

On an existential level, talk is cheap, and money speaks. In politics, the only two public metrics for measuring a candidate's strength are the money they raise and their vote total on Election Day.

The truth is, nine times out of ten, the better-financed campaign will win—after all, someone with more money has more resources to spend on voter contact, can get in front of more people, and has convinced more people to give to their race. You can guarantee someone who's donated to a campaign is going to vote; after all, he or she has some skin in the game.

Don't let anyone trick you. You probably can't raise all your money online.

You're not Barack Obama or Bernie Sanders. You aren't going to have an email list with millions of people on it and you're probably not going to be one of the few candidates whose story gets picked up by reporters, goes viral across the internet, and draws the attention of grassroots donors all across the country.

■ **Grassroots donors:** A term politicos use to mean small-dollar donors, usually folks giving $10, $50, or $100 at a time, usually online. It's cheesy jargon. I wish I had another word; I don't.

There is no magical way to raise money online. Bernie Sanders didn't tap into some special tech toolbox or do anything fancy—in fact, his message was simple: If you supported him, you showed it by contributing and joining his movement. President Obama did the same thing in 2008 and 2012. And for what it's worth: More than three million people donated to Hillary Clinton, too.

What these campaigns have in common is that they made it clear that if you wanted to be a part of what the candidates were building, you donated. People didn't give because of any particular tactic or even broader digital strategy; it was all about the candidate.

Be you. Be authentic. If your story picks up traction online, great—have an easy way for people who care about your race to give. But the truth is, as you do to achieve all important things, you're going to have to work to raise the money.

First, start by learning the rules.

Campaign finance regulations are a hellscape.

In many races, you can't raise or spend more than a specific amount (sometimes as little as $1,000) before triggering filing and reporting requirements. For example, it may be the case that you need to appoint a treasurer and form a candidate committee before accepting any contributions or pledges.

Knowing the rules will help you determine when to publicly launch your campaign, name a treasurer, and begin actively fundraising. Also, obviously, knowing the rules will keep you from breaking them.

You can find the rules in the same place you found the guidelines on how to file. If you're not sure, call the clerk or administrator of elections and ask. It's better to err on the safe side regarding this.

Once you know the fundraising rules that govern your campaign, you can use them to help determine the timing of your launch—the rules often create a domino effect. For example, let's say the rules require you to appoint a treasurer or create a candidate committee within two weeks of accepting any contributions. This, combined with the fact that most campaign documents are made public right away, will likely indicate a time frame for launch.

There are some tools you can use to raise money as part of conditional fundraising (as in: People pledge to give if you decide to run). You could launch an online campaign to create a fund for a potential run—but it's much harder to do that before you've legitimately launched, so you may be setting yourself up for failure. Think seriously about whether you're ready to have your dreams crushed before you even make an effort.

When you scope out the fundraising rules, find out what disclaimer language you'll need to put on your contribution forms as well as what information you need to collect from donors. Usually it's the donor's full name, address, employer, and occupation, but some states or jurisdictions may want even more.

Your state may require you to include the legal rules for giving, your campaign's physical address, and the name of your treasurer. Don't mess that up.

If your treasurer has to be listed in your disclaimer, you need to pick someone who won't leave you open to any scandalous stories. Ideally, your treasurer is well connected in the community and is willing to help fundraise.

Double-check for any restrictions on your treasurer. For example, in some states you cannot serve as a treasurer if you are a treasurer for another candidate committee.

Other things to look up: Compliance regulations. Once you start collecting money, you usually trigger reporting deadlines—times at which you have to report all income to the governing election administrator. Depending on your race, you may also be required to report pledges. The rules associated with these reports are very extensive. Depending on your campaign budget, you might want to hire a compliance firm to file these reports, as it is very important that they are accurate and filed in a timely manner.

Ultimately, understanding the requirements is your job. Do not fuck it up.

Public financing might be an option.

In some states or cities, the election administrators have set up public financing for campaigns. If a candidate can raise a certain amount of money at a certain level of donation from residents of that state or city, the district will match those donations, often at a higher rate; in some places it's as much as six to one. If your campaign takes public financing, your spending is capped at a particular amount.

Public financing is awesome. These systems give real people a greater voice in elections by incentivizing candidates to build out broad donor bases in order to have access to the public funding. They bring more people into the process and reduce the reliance on rich supporters and on special interests. Public financing makes it easier for people without wealthy networks to run for office—that means our government can be more representative of the citizens.

There are often specific rules around reporting that come into play if you participate in the public finance program; make sure your team is prepared to handle those.

If public financing is available in your race, you'll have to decide for yourself whether you want to take it. (My two cents: Why the fuck not?)

LEARN MORE ON THE INTERNET Google "[YOUR STATE]" + "campaign public financing."

Get your fundraising operations in order.

I talked about this a bit as one of the twelve steps to take before you run, but make sure you've got a good system in place for tracking donors and donations. An Excel spreadsheet might cut it, but you should consider licensing out a tool like NGP VAN (yes, the same NGP VAN that does the voter file), which is set up for exporting compliant donor reporting.

Identify a system for online fundraising (Democrats tend to use ActBlue, but there are other options out there) and make sure the data all feeds into the same system.

Figure out your process for both donor outreach and follow-up. When someone enters your donor universe, who's the first one to reach out? How does that communication get tracked? Once someone gives, who gets notified in order to send a thank-you note and how? Who's in charge of thank-you notes?

You can set up a volunteer fundraising team to help you coordinate these operations; a good database helps.

Determine who to ask for money.

The obnoxious answer is "everyone." The more realistic answer is "a few tiers of people."

The first people you ask for money will be your friends and family. Remember how, back on page 87, you were told to make a list of everyone you know? These are the people you'll go to on day one to help springboard your campaign. Then they'll become your best advocates.

If you're embarrassed to ask your friends and family for money, remember:

It's not for *you*. You're not asking for a handout. You're asking them to invest in their community and in your hometown's future.

You can also look into getting funding from issue groups. Start with the folks most aligned with your message, then folks who might have one particular thing in common—then don't forget to ask the people who hate your opponent.

Progressives can look up communities like Daily Kos, MoveOn, Democracy for America, the Progressive Change Campaign Committee, or Our Revolution. Pro-choice women can check out EMILY's List; LGBT Americans can look up the Victory Institute; African Americans should search for the Collective PAC, and Latinos should check out the Latino Victory Project. That's just the big ones! There are groups for nearly every demographic (and sub-demographic) if you search hard enough. They literally exist to support you: Make it easy for them to find you.

LEARN MORE ON THE INTERNET Google "[DEMOGRAPHIC]" + "[YOUR PARTY]" + "[PAC]."

This might require some political finesse and often a bit of strategic communication with the staff and members in a PAC, but it can yield a good return. Look at the candidates the PACs tend to endorse and find the ones with whom you have something in common. Again, you can decide not to take money from PACs if you don't want to. That's your campaign's call.

The party might have a list of known donors in your area, or they might have nothing at all. There is literally no "magic list" of donors you can just ping and they'll spit out checks. Donors—like voters and like you—are real people who decide on a case-by-case basis whom they want to contribute to.

After you have gone through your initial connections, focus your donor targets on those local to you first, by region and then by state. People are far more likely to give to candidates near them than to those in races they don't think impact them.

WHO YOU TAKE MONEY FROM

We can—and should—have a larger debate about the flood of big money in politics. (Per usual: Want to fix it? Run for office, win, and propose legislation to change it.)

But in an uncharacteristically idealistic opinion, I think it is deeply cynical to assume that any single politician is swayed by the donors they attract. Yes, some are, and you should certainly follow the money; when a politician votes a certain way on a bill, look and see who their donors are.

Realistically, it's more of a chicken-and-egg scenario. Did that politician vote that way because of their donors? Or did those donors give to that candidate because he or she held those positions in the first place? Sure, money has sway—it's harder for a politician to change his or her mind when donors have invested for a particular reason—but it is not as simple as "money buys votes."

You have to decide for yourself what kind of people you want to take money from. Donors above a certain level will be disclosed, and your opponent will likely poke through your donor list to look for bad stories to drop on you about the kind of people you associate with. You alone can determine your risk tolerance.

WHO DOES THE ASKING

You. You need to do the asking. You can't outsource this. Donor contact and voter contact are similar in that you're the best advocate for your campaign and your passion.

If your partner or spouse is willing to fundraise for you, they'd be a great advocate, too. They know you better than anyone and can speak about you in a personal way.

Your friends and family are also good surrogates. Your goal is to be seen as someone other people are getting behind—when friends fundraise for you, they're lending you their credibility.

OTHER WAYS TO RAISE MONEY

Email is the king of online fundraising—you can target and personalize, all within a platform where people are used to dealing with money. (Think: e-commerce.) Your website should prioritize email sign-ups for this reason: Once someone joins your list, they're automatically a donor prospect.

You can send email through your list; you can also provide a sample copy for friends and family to use to email their friends and ask them to give.

Text message programs can also be lucrative if you have the money to spend on sending out texts and can set up a text-to-give program.

You can also send good old-fashioned snail mail. You could do direct-mail fundraising through a consulting firm or finance consultant, but this could be a great thing to have volunteers do. Ask them to write personal notes to friends and family, explaining why they're supporting your campaign and why their friends should too. The personal touch will go a long way.

DIALING FOR DOLLARS

Any candidate who wants to win will spend a good chunk of the day doing "call time"—literally picking up the phone and cold-calling donor prospects. You might start with your personal Rolodex; then you might move to people who sign up on your website, friends of friends, and any donor leads you can wrangle. You should also call anyone who gives to your campaign to thank them.

Whether you do this on your personal phone or use a Google Voice number is up to you. Keep in mind: If you use your personal cell phone, then people actually have your cell phone number. You decide whether you care about that.

Be consistent. You should set aside time every day for call time. The more you do it, the better you'll get at it.

Lots of candidates complain about call time. Those candidates have a bad attitude. Don't be one of them. You want to win? This is what it takes: asking people to invest in your campaign and in their own future. Pick up the phone and stop complaining.

HOLD IN-PERSON EVENTS

In-person events are a great way to give someone an experience in exchange for their donation and to reinforce that when they give, they're joining a community of people who share their values.

Don't be afraid to do something a little wacky when it comes to fundraising events. Some ideas . . .

- Picnics
- Trivia nights
- Pie-the-politician events
- BBQ-making contest
- Happy hours
- Movie nights
- Local concerts
- Pancake breakfast
- Races (where people run on your behalf)
- Afternoons at the dog park
- Karaoke nights
- Bowling contests

For any given event, you can set a range of ticket prices. If you're going to host an event for low-dollar donors (less than $50), consider pairing it with a higher-dollar reception beforehand, and a mid-dollar reception after. Use your time wisely! It's one of your most precious resources.

Host committees are common for events—people commit to "write or raise" a certain amount (meaning: contribute directly or find other people to give smaller amounts, which add up to the total amount) and often help cover the overhead costs of the event, like food or the venue. They're responsible for getting guests in the door. By putting host-committee members on the public invitation, you hold them accountable for a successful event and also create a little bit of FOMO (fear of missing out).

Try to keep event overhead low. Yes, you have to spend money to make money, but don't go overboard. Use volunteers to staff your fundraising events, and don't serve filet mignon when hamburgers will do.

SELLING MERCHANDISE

Big campaigns often sell T-shirts, pins, stickers, and more. Unless you've got big name recognition, most people won't want to wear your name on their chest. Consider getting a few dozen shirts printed for volunteers, but don't plan on selling these for any kind of profit.

For bumper stickers and pins—if you decide to get them, give them to donors as thank-you gifts. You can stick them in the mail with your thank-you notes, which you're obviously sending because your mother taught you manners and you're not some kind of monster.

WHAT YOU SHOULD KNOW ABOUT DONOR PSYCHOLOGY

A few things to keep in mind as you shape your fundraising pitches . . .

Donating and voting work according to the same psychology—no one likes to vote if they're the only one voting, and no one likes to donate if they're the only one giving. You need to create a sense of FOMO. Show momentum. That's why campaigns will often tout their number of donors.

The person most likely to give today is the person who gave yesterday. The psychological hurdle from non-donor to donor is big; the one from donor to repeat donor is small. You know the expression "In for a penny, in for a pound"? If someone gives you even $1, they're investing in you. They're getting some skin in the game, and if you maintain that relationship, you'll be able to get more money from them over time. You've crossed the biggest hurdle of convincing them you're worth giving money to—now you just have to move that needle on how much.

Urgency matters. People fucking love a deadline. They'll procrastinate until you give them a reason to cough up the money. Fortunately, you have deadlines built into your campaign. You have legitimate filing dates, after which you have to report the amount you've raised for public record. People (meaning press and your opponents) really do look at those public filings as a sign of your campaign's strength. Lean into those deadlines and remind people that if they want to support your campaign at a moment that matters, they need to give before those key dates.

Set public goals, explain why they aren't arbitrary numbers, and show progress toward those goals. Then break those goals down into "micro goals" to make them achievable. For example:

"I need to raise $2,000 by this Friday to pay for printing new campaign literature so I can hand it out when I go canvassing next week. I'm looking for fifteen people in your neighborhood to get us over the top. Will you give $50 to help us hit our goal?"

There's a concept in organizing called "theory of change"—this is a jargony way of saying that it's important to explain how and why what you're asking someone to do will matter. Connect the dots between A and Z and don't assume anything. Don't just say "donate." It's "donate to help pay for X—X matters because it will help us reach more voters." If what you're asking someone to do for your campaign doesn't have a clear theory of change, perhaps it's not worth asking them to do.

Ask people for more than you think they can give. The worst thing that can happen is they say no. The second worst thing that can happen is they say, "No, but I can give [insert an amount a little bit less than what you requested]." Don't be coy.

Folks who give are giving because they agree with your values and vision for where you want to take your community. Depending on how much they donate, their name and information may be a part of the public record. Lean into that—voting is private but whether they give is public; ask if someone wants to be known as on your side.

HOW TO ACTUALLY MAKE THE ASK

So you've got a donor prospect on the phone—great. Start by telling the person about yourself and why you're running. This is just like canvassing: Introduce yourself, tell your story, and ask them what they care about. Be a real human who gives a shit about someone else; listen when people talk, and actively engage with them.

Find a way to connect what they care about to your race. Show how you share their values. Talk about the importance of your campaign and how you're running your organization. Explicitly ask for a specific amount of money.

Then—and this is key—shut the fuck up.

You'll be tempted to keep talking. Don't. Sit on your hands if you have to. Take a drink of water. Sing a song in your head.

This isn't an auction or a negotiation. Just shut your mouth and wait for them to speak. Maybe they'll say no. Maybe they'll say, "No, not that amount, but maybe less," or, "Not yet, but can you reach back out in a few weeks." Whatever happens, you've got a starting point for building a relationship.

At the end of the call, be grateful, and for the love of God, say thank you. Ask if there's anyone else they think you should talk to, and if they offer up some names, ask for introductions.

Follow-up is key.

Whether or not they donate, make sure you keep track of who you talk to and when, and what they care about.

Reach out regularly, as you have campaign updates to provide. Land a great press story? Knock on an astounding number of doors? Send an email to the donor prospects you've met with, plus anyone who's donated, to show them what their donation is helping—or could help to—yield.

Anything you put in writing to a donor or donor prospect could and will be forwarded along to someone else. Be aware.

Once someone gives: Always, always, always say thank you.

Handwrite notes to say thank you. Put them in the mail. Get your operations tight so that if someone gives on a Monday, they get a thank-you call on a Tuesday and a thank-you note in the mail the following week.

You could have different thank-you processes for a $5 donor versus a $500 donor, and perhaps you could mix it up between online and on the phone—but generally speaking, the more personal and more labor-intensive for you, the more of an impact it'll have on the donor.

There is no such thing as showing too much gratitude.

Launch day matters.

Your launch day will be a huge moment for your fundraising—it's a chance to pick the low-hanging fruit, so make sure you've got your shit together before you go live.

Before you kick off your campaign, make sure you've got a functioning website with a way to take sign-ups and donations, and a printable PDF version of a donation form with all the relevant information. You'll also need a "one-pager"—a quick and dirty summary of who you are and why you're running. It should include contact info for your campaign, where to sign up and donate, and a photo of you!

Some donors might ask for a "deck" or a PowerPoint slide show on what your campaign is about. It's good to have one that's well-designed and easy to update and share as a PDF, but you don't need that before you launch.

Jump to page 162 for a quick list of what else you need to do before you launch.

A WORD ON FINANCE CONSULTANTS

You might get told you need to hire finance consultants or vendors to help you raise money. These folks will help you set up a finance committee structure and could introduce you to some major donors in your state or district. However, they're not replacements for your own efforts. At the end of the day, you have to make the ask and be compelling. In some races, these consultants might bring value—in statewide races, maybe, or possibly a big state legislature race. If you can't afford one, don't worry about it.

You can do this!

Raising money doesn't need to be scary. You can do this with some hustle and some chutzpah. Just keep in mind: You're not begging. You're asking people who share your values to invest in themselves and in their future. You'll do the hard work. All they have to do is help you.

Fundraising can be demoralizing; you're going to get rejected a lot. Keep in mind, when people say no to you, it's nearly never about *you*. Maybe they can't afford to give right now, or maybe they're not the primary decision-maker about finances in their home. Or maybe they only give to certain causes, or certain types of people, or certain races.

Make a compelling case, show you're using money wisely and effectively, and make it easy for people to give if they decide to contribute.

You've got to put yourself out there. You won't get money you don't ask for! And if you really want to win, you need the money.

9
WRITING YOUR CAMPAIGN PLAN

■ **Once you've wrapped your** head around all the various options and gotten the lay of the land, you have to write a campaign plan. Even if your plan changes, it's important to put pen to paper (or fingers to keyboard to Google Docs) and outline your strategy. Your team needs a guiding vision, and you need to know how the small choices you're making fit into the big picture.

There is no one way to write a campaign plan—organize it the way it makes sense in your head. I've included below a possible template with questions you'll want to answer, either in writing or as you go. Some of this might not be relevant to your campaign, and you might not have all the answers right away. That's okay! It's good to identify "open questions" where you need to figure things out.

Each of the "departments" I've listed is really a function you need to account for, set objectives for, and define which tactics you'll use to accomplish the goals you need to hit. Always come back to your key focus: Talking to the voters you need in order to win. Anything outside of that is either bonus or a poor use of your resources, depending on your fundraising and time limitations. Always have a metric you can measure your success by, and schedule regular points to check in against those metrics—whether or not you're hitting them and whether or not they're still the right metrics to be measuring. (Possible metrics could be "doors knocked on" or "political groups connected with" or "donors called"—literally anything!) There is no harm in measuring too much. You can decide to ignore what you see in those numbers, but collecting them will help you make informed decisions about your time, your campaign's resources, and your strategy.

Your plan will be a living, breathing, ever-updating document. As you bring on staff or volunteers and deputize them to be in charge of different functions, ask them to write plans, too, on the specifics of what they want to accomplish and how they plan to accomplish it. It's fun for folks to dream big, and they should—but make sure you're focusing your time on things you can actually execute on, even if the path to execution is hard.

Overview

Give a brief outline of your race. What's the district like? What is your opponent like? When is the election?

....

....

....

....

....

....

Why are you running?

Explain why you're running and what kind of campaign you want to run.

....

....

....

....

....

....

Win numbers

Articulate your win number and the research you used to get there. Show your work!

....

....

....

....

....

....

Message frame

Draw your message box for you and each of your opponents.

Candidate: ....

....

....

....

....

WHAT YOU SAY ABOUT YOURSELF	WHAT THEY SAY ABOUT THEMSELVES
WHAT YOU SAY ABOUT YOUR OPPONENT	**WHAT YOUR OPPONENT SAYS ABOUT YOU**

For each of the following departments, make sure you identify who is in charge, who they report to, and what their metrics of success are.

Communications: Press

What is your press plan? What are the major press outlets? How do you, the candidate, engage with the press? Who's authorized to speak on the campaign's behalf? What is the process for pitching press? What's your current press list? How will you keep track of earned media? When will you roll out policy plans? When will you schedule events?

....

....

....

....

....

Communications: Message

What are the key points of the campaign's message? What events will you create to help get that message out (i.e., roundtables, town halls, etc.)? Who is responsible for writing and approving advertising, if any? What is your planned calendar for your message?

....

....

....

....

....

Digital

How does digital fit into the organizing, fundraising, and messaging goals of the campaign? Who is responsible for what? What are the available channels and how do your vote goals align with those channels? How much will you spend on online advertising? Who is in charge of that?

....

....

....

....

....

Fundraising

Who are your target donors? How much do you think you can raise from your immediate network? What are your goals and by what date do you need to hit them in order to pay your bills? Who is accountable for those goals?

....
....
....
....
....
....

Organizing

What are you asking people to do, when are you asking people to do it, and why does it matter? What are your voter contact goals? What is your structure for volunteers?

....
....
....
....
....
....

Political

What is your plan for reaching out to elected officials, outside groups, and others? What are your target groups and who do you need help to reach?

....
....
....
....
....
....

Policy

Who is responsible for deciding policy proposals? What outside help will you get in writing your plans? How will you prioritize?

....

....

....

....

....

....

Research

What self-research have you done? What kind of opposition research will you do? How will you handle any problems? Who is in charge of this?

....

....

....

....

....

....

Scheduling

How does an event get on your calendar? Who handles RSVPs for you? How do you decide between conflicting events? What are the big events you need to be sure to prioritize?

....

....

....

....

....

....

Operations

Who has access to the bank account? Who has a credit card? Who is in charge of filing paperwork? Who works with the lawyers? Who oversees the campaign budget and approves expenses?

....

....

....

....

....

....

GOTV

What are the different ways people vote in your community? How does your program interact with those different types of voting? What are you asking people to do?

....

....

....

....

....

....

Timeline and milestones

Aggregate everything you've written out so far and put it into one calendar, including important legal deadlines, fundraising deadlines, any scheduled debates or big events you know are coming, voter registration and balloting deadlines, and anything else you need to have your eyes on.

....

....

....

....

....

....

Campaign structure

Draw your pyramid chart. Who is doing what? Who reports to whom? What positions are for volunteers and which are for paid staff?

Campaign budget

Detail exactly what you're going to spend your money on. Make sure you note the known-unknowns.

CHECKLIST BEFORE LAUNCH

- ☐ Confirm filing deadlines and fundraising requirements.
- ☐ Prepare basic website that can intake email addresses and money.
- ☐ Get social media accounts ready to launch.
- ☐ Get political outreach done. (Have you given a heads-up to the right people?)
- ☐ Plan for press outreach. (What reporters are you reaching out to first? How are you notifying people? What outlets do you want to be in?)
- ☐ Get your Rolodex in order. (Who are you going to call first for money?)

Make Local Elections Great Again

by Addisu Demissie

National Voter Outreach and Mobilization Director of Hillary for America,
cofounder of 50+1 Strategies

■ **I've worked on three presidential campaigns,** managed a United States Senate campaign, and spent most of my adult life in Washington, DC. But I'm here to tell you that some of the most fun I've ever had, the best professional training I've ever received, and the most meaningful work I've ever done has been on local races. As a consultant to candidates for mayor, county supervisor, and school board, I've been able to hone my skills, experiment with different strategies and, most important, see firsthand the difference a single, driven candidate can make on their campaign and their community.

Okay, I just read that last paragraph back and I understand why you might think I'm full of it. But if you're considering running for local office or working on a local campaign, bear with me for a few hundred more words. I hope you'll agree.

Here are four simple reasons why I think you should Run for Something—locally:

1. *Local government does more than you might think.*

It's easy to gratuitously diss Congress, but I'm not here for that; members and their staffs do important work both in terms of policy-making and constituent service. That said, it's undeniable that it's hard to pass significant reforms in a 535-person national legislature, especially in our hyper-partisan political environment. Not to mention, the policy and political debates that do take place in Washington are typically at a more abstract level than those happening in your neighborhood grocery store or over dinner with your family and friends.

The thing about city councils, county boards of supervisors, and local executive officers like mayors and district attorneys is that, when it comes to most issues— from potholes to public transportation, from public safety to public schools—they actually have more power and authority over the day-to-day experiences of people in your community than anyone in Washington, DC does. And that responsibility, paired with the literal proximity that elected officials have to their voters and constituents, pressures local government to actually do more with that power and authority, for better or for worse.

A lot of people think running for local office means starting at the bottom of the ladder. I think that's total nonsense. If you're a person who cares intensely about your community and wants to get shit done, there's literally no better position from which to do that than as an elected official in local government.

2. *You get to run the kind of campaign you want to run.*

Here's the dirty little secret about running local campaigns: there's no real playbook for it. Sure, there are some guidelines that it would be smart to follow— that's why you picked up this book, after all, and why folks like me are in business— but in the end, there are too many differences between localities, regions, and offices to suggest that a campaign for city council in the urban northeast, district attorney in the rural south, or county executive in the exurban midwest should have much in common. Local consultants help, but you, as the candidate, are usually the most knowledgeable about the message, the strategy, and the tactics that will be most successful in your community. That's even true of first-time candidates. You should be confident in that fact, and with that confidence comes the freedom to test your theory of change, try new things, and emphasize the issues that you care about most. It's liberating and, in my experience, what makes those campaigns especially fun.

3. *With passion and effort, you can win.*

I'm going to try hard not to turn this into a self-help pep talk here, but if you take one thing away from this little essay, let it be this: you don't have to have a particular résumé, background, or skill set to run for any office—and local office in particular. Everyone has to start somewhere; I worked with one first-time candidate who barely paid attention to politics before getting inspired to run for school board because no one else was challenging a two-term incumbent who was literally verbally abusing colleagues at board meetings. He won. Four years later, he became the board president and is being recruited to run for other city offices. This story is normal!

What were his secrets? First, he had a real passion for education policy. The lesson: don't pick the office you want to run for, pick the issues in which you want to make a difference and then find the office that can help you make that difference. I guarantee you there is at least one local office—at the state, county, city, or even neighborhood level—that has a perhaps surprising amount of say over public policy in that area.

Second, he put in the work. The real work of campaigning is dialing for dollars, knocking on doors, and showing up basically everywhere you can to build support among your neighbors and community members. I cannot stress enough how important this is to running and winning local campaigns, way more so than those at the federal level, in my opinion. The lesson: in local campaigns, you can put yourself into position to win through sheer effort; the costs are lower, the electorate is smaller, the races are generally less partisan and, most important, voters always respect the hustle.

4. *Win or lose, you'll be better for it.*

No one runs for office with the intention of losing, but there are certainly good reasons to run, even if winning isn't likely or even your primary concern. You can use it to elevate an issue, hold an incumbent accountable for a vote or a position that you find objectionable, or even just to position yourself for a future run when you're more ready personally or professionally to give it your all. I've worked on dozens of winning and losing local campaigns and I have yet to find a candidate who did not improve over the course of a campaign—as a public speaker, an advocate, a fundraiser, a coalition builder, and a *citizen*. Running for office is work, no doubt, but it also will give you skills you might not have known you needed and make you a better public servant in your community, no matter what form that takes going forward.

10
SO YOU'RE NOT RUNNING FOR OFFICE
(YET)

■ **So you've decided not to run for office.** (Or at least you're putting it off for now.) I forgive you—mostly.

But you can't let not being a candidate excuse you from giving a shit about politics. Democracy is a participatory sport—if you want something out of your government, you've got to step up and be a part of the process.

There are a number of ways you can do that.

> " *Believing in the cause is why I showed up to volunteer, but asking people to contribute their time and money was something I had to learn. Eventually, I realized campaigns actually offer people the opportunity to make a change to their own lives and become leaders in their community.*"
>
> —ROBBY MOOK, Campaign Manager for Hillary for America and Executive Director of the DCCC, on the personal benefits of volunteering

You should volunteer on a political campaign.

Volunteers are the backbone, spine, arms, legs, heart, and soul of any campaign. It is no exaggeration to say that a campaign literally can't function without people volunteering their time. Person-to-person communication is how a candidate wins—and you can help with that.

There are different ways to volunteer, depending on what kind of person you are and what you feel most comfortable with.

———————

Does any of this describe you? You're a schmoozer. You're the kind of person who sits down on a flight next to a stranger and deplanes with someone's phone number to get drinks next time you're in the same city. (Not in a creepy way, in a new-friend kind of way.) You can always find something in common with people you meet. You like walking outside and racking up steps on your Fitbit.

Or maybe you're not as mobile, or your allergies may keep you from spending hours outside. You'd rather be in the office with some friends, dialing away. You're comfortable speaking to strangers over the phone.

If the first describes you, you should canvass for your chosen candidate; if the second describes you, you should make calls.

How to actually do it: Start by checking out the campaign's website. See if they've got a place to sign up to volunteer—if they do, sign up! They might also list the upcoming canvasses and phone banks you can help with. If not, find contact info for the campaign. (Usually there's a generic email address or a phone number you can call.)

You should also look up the candidate on Facebook, since some campaigns will post their volunteer events there to reach as many people as possible. RSVP for the event that makes the most sense for your schedule and that fits your interests.

Bigger campaigns might make confirmation calls or emails to follow up with you and confirm that you're going to show up when you said you would.

Campaigns usually expect a pretty sizable flake rate, since often up to half of people who RSVP will not follow through.

Be one of the people who show up. That will automatically make you in the top decile of volunteers for that campaign. (It's true what they say: Eighty percent of success is simply showing up.)

When you arrive at the event, you'll be asked to sign in. If it's a paper sign-in sheet, write legibly so whoever does data entry doesn't have to struggle to read your chicken scratch. If it's on a computer or tablet, make sure there are no typos.

If you're canvassing, make sure you're wearing comfortable shoes, sunscreen, or whatever weather gear you need, and that you're prepped for a stroll outside. When you get to the canvass launch (which might be the campaign's office or might be a meeting place out in the community), an organizer or volunteer captain will set you up with a buddy (maybe a friend, maybe a stranger-about-to-be-a-friend) and a walk packet. That walk packet will have maps, directions, and a script, and you'll probably get a clipboard and pens in order to take notes on your conversations. You'll get trained regarding what to say, how to fill out the sheets, and what to do with any weird questions. You might get handed some campaign literature to give out or leave at the door of anyone who doesn't answer.

If you're making calls, you should bring headphones (if you prefer to talk on the phone using those), a phone charger, and possibly your laptop—check with the campaign regarding whether they want you to use a computer or not. The organizer or volunteer captain will show you where to sit, set you up with a phone (or ask if you're comfortable using your own phone), and give you a call sheet, a script, and a way to take notes. You'll plop down in a chair, pick up the phone, and start dialing.

Don't be afraid to ask questions. The organizers and campaign staff would rather spend a few extra minutes explaining things before you get started than have you do something incorrectly because your ego was too big to admit you were confused.

When taking notes or filling out call sheets, be thorough, be clear, and use good handwriting. Complete your call sheets or walk packets—don't leave something half-done, because it'll be harder for someone else to pick up where you left off.

Your goal should be to make things easier for everyone else. If what you're doing might make more work for someone else, then you're doing the wrong thing. A campaign's most precious resources are time and human capacity; don't waste either of those things.

■ Shift: A term campaigns use to mean a block of time they're scheduling volunteers. A shift might last for one hour, or it might last for three. If you can, stay for a whole shift. If you can't, that's okay—just communicate that to the organizer you RSVP'd with.

At the end of your shift, make sure to return all your sheets and sign out with the organizer. If they're good, they'll ask you to sign up for another shift before you leave. Do that. Don't fuck around and say you'll sign up online later. Just put it on your calendar before you walk out the door.

Keep coming back. The volunteers campaigns love are the reliable ones. If you keep showing up when you say you will and doing the work, you'll quickly rise in the ranks. After establishing a reputation as a good volunteer, you might get asked to take on a leadership role. You might get asked to train other volunteers, or organize events yourself, or even one day, become a campaign "fellow" or "intern" to put the title on your résumé. If a campaign has the budget to hire staff, they often turn to their best volunteers first, because those are people who've proven they'll do the work.

If you don't have a good experience, make sure to say something to the organizers. Explain why it wasn't great and why you don't think you'll be returning. An organizer can't improve unless they get that kind of feedback.

Take photos of what you're doing and post them on Instagram, Twitter, or Facebook. Tag the candidate or use the hashtag they want you to use; you will likely get shared by the campaign as they try to show there's enthusiasm for the race. (Welcome to being a political prop. Embrace it.)

Congratulations. By helping with voter contact, you're making a real, tangible, measurable impact on a campaign. You're doing the hard work that actually wins or loses races. You're not just bitching on the internet; you're making a difference.

Does any of this describe you? You're always the one in your friend group who makes plans, picks restaurants, makes the reservations, handles the travel details, and ensures that everyone has the information they need. You *love* finding cheap deals and are scrappy, making good use of your resources. You're a pro at handling grumpy customer-service representatives.

If so, consider helping with scheduling and advance.

Not all campaigns have this as a volunteer opportunity, but bigger races (and definitely presidential campaigns) will be looking for folks to help get their schedule tight and run smooth events.

Advance teams are tasked with making sure the logistics of an event are handled. When you do advance (yes, it's both a noun and a verb), you'll be helping scope out locations, figure out security, deal with where the press might go, figure out travel and accommodations for the candidate and staff, and deal with details big and small, like Wi-Fi, water, and snacks.

How to actually do it: Big campaigns will have staff who head up advance teams; reach out via email or phone and ask if you can volunteer. Small campaigns won't have anyone in charge of this but will appreciate the help.

If you're able to do this, don't say you can do it and then back out. This is the kind of work that needs some follow-through; if you agree to help "advance" an event, the campaign is counting on you to actually do it. If you can't go 100 percent, this is not a volunteer task for you.

Does any of this describe you? You're a wizard with Excel. You know how formulas work and can make a pivot table in your sleep. Or you pick up new tech software quickly and easily, without too many hiccups. Or, you find mindless work soothing because you can put in your headphones, listen to a podcast, and zone out while you type repetitive information over and over again.

If so, data entry is for you.

Campaigns collect massive amounts of data—everything from info on who signs in at events to phone numbers to voter registration info to what happens in conversations during canvasses and phone-bank calls.

That information is only useful if it gets added back to the campaign's voter file. (Check the appendix for a quick description on what the voter file is.)

How to actually do it: For a small campaign, once again, just offer yourself up. Call or email the team and say explicitly, "I want to help you do data entry." They'll trip over themselves getting you in the door.

For big campaigns, you're better off stopping by the office in person and letting someone know how you want to help.

To be a rock star, schedule a specific time every week that you can come in and do data entry. Knowing you're available and reliable will relieve them of serious amounts of stress and anxiety over how and when data will get entered. (It's not unusual for organizers to be in the office from 9 p.m. until 1 a.m. entering data every night after volunteers do phone banks.)

You'll get set up with a log-in for whatever voter file database the campaign uses and told exactly what to enter where. Just follow instructions and make sure you save your work often.

Does any of this describe you? You love baking, cooking, and providing comfort to friends when they're stressed out. You're a pro at keeping schedules organized and making sure the details are handled—you've got your eyes out for empty coffeepots or printers that need new ink. You get a thrill out of making sure people are happy, fed, and caffeinated. You've got some spare room in your home and you like having guests.

If so, you're a perfect comfort captain, office manager, or host for supporter housing.

How to actually do this: Each of these volunteer roles is slightly different, but all are equally important.

Comfort captain is a real title that has real responsibilities. Organizers and volunteers can get so busy and work such long hours that sometimes they forget to eat, or they don't have time to eat, or both. (On the 2016 presidential campaign, we often pulled off the Seamless hat trick—ordering delivery for all three meals.) Comfort captains ensure that no one realizes it's 8 p.m. and the reason people are snapping at each other is not actually annoyance but rather the more pernicious enemy called "hanger." Comfort captains help organize volunteers to bring by food and snacks, and make sure the office coffee supply is stocked. Comfort captains may be asked to provide one meal a week, or a month, or become part of a rotation of folks during GOTV weekend. Not all heroes wear capes; comfort captains are heroes.

Office managers help run broader office operations. Maybe an office manager sits at the welcome desk, answers phones, and makes sure people sign in. Or maybe the office manager is responsible for keeping an eye on office supplies, doing Office Depot runs, and keeping the Wi-Fi up and running. A campaign might have a rotation of office managers led by an office director, who ensures there's always someone to open the doors in the morning and lock the doors at night. There should never be folks at the office without an office manager there to oversee things (and who knows where the secret stash of Diet Coke is). Office managers are also heroes.

Supporter housing is the secret source of a campaign's power. Volunteers and staff often come from out of state or out of town, especially on bigger campaigns. Supporter housing gives those folks a place to stay. Sometimes supporter housing can last for a weekend; other times supporter housing can last for months or even a year. Organizers don't make much money and often arrive or leave at a moment's notice; not having to deal with paying rent, signing or breaking a lease, and actually moving saves an organizer a huge headache and a lot of income. Most organizers aren't really home that often—they'll show up after 11 p.m. to go to sleep, and leave at 7 a.m. to start a day of one-on-ones. If you're housing an organizer, you probably won't notice the difference. You can host as many or as few folks as you have room for, and for as long as you are able to. Supporters who host organizers and volunteers are also heroes. (Campaigns have a lot of heroes.)

For any of these roles, simply reach out to your local organizer on the campaign and offer yourself up for these positions. They'll be grateful for your help.

Does this describe you? You're a prolific social media user. You tweet a lot, you're all up in people's Facebook newsfeeds, and your Instagram stories are heart-wrenching tales with stars, villains, and puppies. Or you've got a big audience, just by having been online for a while, and folks who follow you are hyper-engaged. Or you're an amazing iPhone photographer and you know how to make a badass Boomerang.

If so, you should help out as a "grassroots tweeter."

How to actually do it: Reach out to the campaign through their website or social media accounts and ask: Do they have a program for getting talking points and messaging to real people online? Big campaigns often have list-servs or chat rooms for people to join, or maybe a Facebook group; smaller ones likely don't have the capacity for this kind of volunteer management.

■ "Grassroots tweeter" is a meaningless phrase that campaigns use when what they really mean is "real person who advocates for us on the internet."

Regardless of whether they do or don't, take your cues from the campaign's primary social media accounts. Retweet and share as much as you can, and when it's relevant, add your own endorsement or viewpoint to give it a personal touch.

I talk a lot of trash about people complaining on the internet, but the truth is, this does matter. By sharing political content, you're helping your candidate in two key ways:

First, you're vouching for the candidate to your friends. People trust recommendations from friends or family more than they do those from the original source. (For example: I might see a book at a bookstore and think it looks interesting. But I'm not going to buy it until my friend tweets about how much she loved it. I use her taste as a heuristic for determining my own interest.) By lending your credibility to the candidate you support, you're helping them reach a broader network.

Second, you're creating a permission structure for other people to also support a candidate—any candidate! You're giving other people an implicit okay to be political, take a side, and publicly represent their chosen candidates. In the post-Trump era, it's certainly more acceptable to be political in public, but some people are still afraid of being actively *for* something, as opposed to *against* something. By putting yourself out there, even in a low-key way, you're opening the door for others to do the same.

Your social media posts could bring someone new into the campaign who could make a difference, whether that's by volunteering, donating, or being the critical vote that tips the balance.

———

Does any of this describe you? You're shameless about asking for things. You're always able to get folks to come around to your point of view. You have a passion for putting on events and like to bring your friends together for a good time. You can't necessarily give a ton of time to a campaign but you'd like to make an impact.

If so, help the campaign raise money as a fundraiser.

One of the best things you can do for a campaign is donate—and then get your friends to donate too. (Remember: Your contribution helps vouch for the campaign in your friends' eyes.) Host an event for the campaign or do an online fundraising drive.

How to actually do it: Call or email the campaign and ask to speak to the finance director. Tell him or her that you want to help the campaign raise money. Be realistic about how much you expect you can raise—think about your network, their relative willingness to invest in causes, and what you feel comfortable asking for.

> ■ Bigger campaigns will have programs where you can "bundle" for the campaign— meaning get a bunch of your friends to donate and you get credit for their involvement. Ask about that.

The campaign may encourage you to set up a page on their fundraising platform and will ensure you get credit for your support.

If you want to host an in-person event, bring that up. Don't expect the candidate to be able to come on a moment's notice, but there is no harm in asking, and if they can't make it work, ask if they can recommend a surrogate to speak at your fundraiser. Pull together a "host committee" to support you, each member of which is responsible for raising a particular amount of money to cover costs and support the candidate. You're building your own little pyramid scheme to make yourself valuable to the candidate. Then find a place, set a date, and invite folks. The campaign may or may not be able to help you in promoting your fundraiser— that's why you need your pyramid scheme.

At your fundraiser, include food and drinks, and have a brief speaking program. Be honest with your friends about why you want them to give to this campaign. Your personal endorsement will go a long way.

For tips on asking for money, head over to page 152.

You should also donate.

This isn't a volunteer activity, but if you can afford to give, you should do it. Even $5 or $10 makes a difference in small races, and campaigns *love* to tout their number of donors—a good campaign will leverage your donation into a story of how people are rallying behind them. You'll become a statistic, but a good one.

After putting even a little bit of money into a race, you'll pay a little more attention. You'll be more aware of how the campaign is going. You'll give a shit just a little bit more.

This is a good thing. You're more likely to vote on Election Day because you've invested in the outcome—not just emotionally but financially.

If you can afford to, set up a recurring donation. There is nothing a campaign loves more than automatic money they can count on and budget around every month.

Ultimately, if you can give something to a campaign, whether it's time, money, snacks, or your credibility, you should do it. Campaigns are driven by the candidate and the campaign staff, but they succeed because of the real people who decide to get involved. If someone inspires you, put your money and time where your heart is and do something about it.

If you're thinking about maybe running for office one day, you should volunteer.

The most important thing you need when you run for office is a good network of people who care about politics and are willing to do the work. By volunteering on a campaign (or at an organization that similarly engages politically active people), you'll get to know other people like you. You'll grow your connections with people who can help you if you decide to run one day.

Sure, it might feel a little slimy to decide to start getting involved in campaigns because you are trying to intentionally build your network for your future career. Whatever. This is how it's done. If you want to win the game, you've got to know how to play it.

Seven Questions

with John Podesta

Chair of Hillary for America | Senior Advisor to Barack Obama | Chief of Staff for Bill Clinton

1. *What's the one-sentence reason why people should run for office?*

Politics and governing are an expression of values and so, if you want the government to reflect your values and if you think you can do the job better than the other guy, run for something.

2. *What (or who) convinced you to get involved in politics the first time?*

My first campaign was the 1968 presidential campaign of Senator Eugene McCarthy, who was running as an opponent of the Vietnam War. The country was in turmoil and politics seemed like the only vehicle to wind down and end the war. Even though we lost and the country elected Richard Nixon, who had a "secret plan to end the war" that was so secret even he didn't know what it was, I got hooked on trying to elect candidates who I thought could make a positive difference for the country.

3. *What was the hardest part of your first campaign?*

I was assigned to organize a small city in Oregon and was handed the keys to a stick-shift car. I never drove stick, but managed to jerk my way up and down mountains for the next two weeks (and we won my city and the primary).

4. *What was the best part of your first campaign?*

I had grown up in a blue-collar neighborhood on the northwest side of Chicago and had never really traveled in America more than two hundred miles from home. From seeing my first palm trees in Los Angeles to the Cascades in Oregon, and from flying in a small plane over Nebraska to working in a storefront in Brooklyn under the shadow of the Verrazano Bridge, I got to see how big, beautiful, and diverse our country really is.

5. *How do you handle losing?*

Sit in a dark room and drink tequila from a bottle.

6. *What should someone do right now if they're thinking about running in five or ten years?*

Get a job on a campaign as an organizer.

7. *What's the best advice someone's given you in relation to working on campaigns?*

Don't let the Russians hack your emails.

11
WHY I MADE CAMPAIGNS A CAREER
(AND WHY YOU SHOULD TOO)

Rule Number One of working on a campaign is simple: Don't make yourself the story.

But because of that, real people (and yes, campaign staffers really do call non-campaign people "real people") don't understand what it's like to live, breathe, sleep, eat, and drink your way through a job that isn't just what you do, but who you are.

I wasn't senior staff on the presidential campaigns I worked on, so I don't have the kind of anecdotes that you might read in campaign tell-alls—stories of riding on *Air Force One*, with sneak peeks behind the curtain at what it's like to be with a candidate, day in and day out.

But the people who really make campaigns run don't have those kinds of stories, either. Ninety-eight percent of campaign staff work at desks, behind computers, or with volunteers. We sit in cavernous offices with less than a single foot of personal space between us, and keep boxes of wine under our feet that we break into each evening as we leave our 9 p.m. daily check-out meetings.

I'm not one of the longtime hacks, but I'm not a rookie either. I've worked three cycles—including two presidential campaigns—starting as an intern in 2011 and ending as a manager of a team of nineteen in 2016. I've raised hundreds of millions of dollars and inspired millions of people to not just care about an election but actually do something about it. I lived in four cities in thirteen months, dragging my sweet terror of a dog across the country with me.

I've taken pay cuts and gotten raises, all while racking up massive amounts of credit card debt. I'm not a crier or a sap, but during campaigns, I've wept on street corners. And while I'm not a hugger (or, honestly, particularly warm and friendly), I've embraced my coworkers in back hallways as they struggled through tough days.

My first campaign was a rush. I showed up at President Obama's reelect HQ, amazed every single day at the people around me. I couldn't believe how lucky I was at twenty-two years old. I felt like I was surrounded by the smartest, most passionate people in America. They let me ghost-write for Barack and Michelle Obama, for celebrities and senators—I even ghost-wrote for Maya Angelou once. I couldn't believe they *let* me stay until 2 a.m. working. It felt like a privilege, not a job. I'd get secretly frustrated by my coworkers, who would complain as if what we were doing was anything less than saving the country and the world.

I remember how on election night, we rode the trolley from HQ to the party and started spraying champagne in the air as we chanted, "Fuck Rafalca," the horse the Romneys owned. (I'm still not sure why.)

My second campaign was harder. I went from being part of a big team to leading a tiny one as I spent eight months in Florida, trying so hard to convince Floridians that they truly did care about health care, raising the minimum wage, and marriage equality.

Florida, as befits its reputation, was pretty weird. I spent a lot of time on the road, driving across the Everglades, often discussing Google advertising or Facebook algorithms with the former governor, Charlie Crist. I got to see a true campaigner in action as he'd shake hands and introduce himself by his first name to everyone he met—janitors, clerks, bankers, and billionaires alike.

Sometimes that campaign was a rush, like the night of the second debate, when our opponent refused to come onstage for seven minutes, leaving our candidate alone on national television, trending nationally on Twitter, and leaving me, the digital director, in charge of our response.

At other moments, it was downright horrific. I spent a very disorienting night in a strip club in Fort Lauderdale as a wealthy donor whispered in my ear, "Take off your panties," and the strippers kept asking me for his credit card, thinking I was "with" him.

Losing that election was painful. We genuinely thought it'd be close, but in a Republican wave election, we couldn't eke it out. Out of twelve million votes, barely 1 percent separated us and the winner. The next day, the entire team went to the office to clean up, then migrated to a local bar to drink margaritas for the next twelve hours. (I will say, if you're going to lose an election, do it in Florida—even in November, the weather is nice and you're near the beach.)

I spent a few weeks in Florida after the election, feeling outraged at every person I met who told me they didn't vote. I wanted to scream at each of them: You're the reason one in four African Americans in Florida can't vote; you're the reason 800,000 people don't have access to affordable health care.

The anger faded after a few weeks, and after a brief stint in DC to rest, I moved to New York. On April 12, we launched Hillary's presidential campaign. After a week of working around the clock and a sleepless night during which we were barely sure the campaign would have a website, I pressed Send on the first email with my fingers shaking and then slid down the wall to the floor, afraid I'd hear someone stampeding through the hallway shouting, "Wait, stop!"

I hired an incredible team that worked constantly. We started having seven-day work weeks around Christmas 2015 and didn't take a day off until the middle of March 2016. I skipped weddings, bachelorette parties, and birthdays. I gave up my dog for six weeks, sending her off to stay with my sister in Philadelphia, and I didn't go to a grocery store in 2016 until midway through April.

That's just how it is during campaigns. Work comes first, always, no exceptions.

I won't sugarcoat this: That primary was fucking brutal, possibly worse than the general. The race got personal, and the back-channeled disputes between the two camps got nasty, which made the victory that much more of a relief. On March 15, the night we swept five states and finally saw the light at the end of the tunnel, we had a dance party in the office that left the place rank with beer soaked into the carpet and wine spilled all over the place. (You can find videos of the party online; a few got played on *Good Morning America* the next day.)

It felt genuinely historic. We were a part of something big, something momentous, and something that could change the lives of millions and millions of people. Even in the exhaustion, the weight of what we were doing never faded too far into the background.

That night, Robby Mook, the campaign manager, gave a speech that someone captured on video. He told us to remember how good that moment felt—because there were going to be hard moments to come. We'd need the good memories to keep us going. We'd need each other, and we'd need to remember: We were fighting for something good and righteous. We might not sleep, or eat a vegetable, or see our families for as long as the campaign lasted, but at the end, it'd be worth it.

We got a lot of pep talks like that during the campaign, spiels on how we were keeping America out of the hands of fascists, or breaking glass ceilings and paving a path for little girls with big dreams. We were fighting for health care for all, for paid family leave, immigration reform, more jobs, and a stronger economy. The fate of the country rested on our shoulders, so we had to work as hard as we could for as long as it took. After the election, the memories of those speeches took on a bitter taste, but at the time, they inspired so many of my colleagues.

I found my inspiration elsewhere. After hearing Hillary's entrance song at every rally, I spent months screaming "Fight Song" by Rachel Platten from the top of my lungs at karaoke bars in Brooklyn and standing on top of desks after debate nights. (I can finally admit it—if you Google a Yahoo! News story from August 2016 about "Fight Song," the final blind quote is mine.) I'd sing one of the verses and clasp my hands to my chest: *It's been two years, I miss my home. A fire burning in my bones, but I still believe.* "This song isn't about Hillary," I would jokingly tell people, "this song is about me."

But the truth is, I really did show up every day for Hillary. I know the popular narrative was that people weren't inspired by her, but I was. I was proud to work for this strong, brave, audacious woman who kept getting knocked down but never knocked out. I believed that if we won, it would be such a fuck-you to every guy who'd ever told me I was too ambitious, too loud, too brash, too much. It was personal to me.

I let that drive me, even when everything else in my life fell apart. The campaign was bad for my health. The stress and the emotional roller coasters of each day were inescapable. I woke up in a cold sweat more nights than not, anxious about what news might have broken when I closed my eyes. Other nights, I'd dream about caucuses in states that didn't have caucuses, about fundraising goals I hadn't hit, or about fights with my coworkers. I didn't sleep much for two years.

We were all sick, all the fucking time. I had a kidney infection at one point, and one girl on my team got shingles. Everyone had a cold, always. My body hurt constantly from eighteen-hour days sitting at a desk. Eating three takeout meals a day left me with a never-fading migraine and constant stomachaches.

And my personal life was a mess. In 2012, I had coworkers who met on the job, dated, and got married a few years after the election—the pressure cooker of a campaign had brought them together, and they found happiness. (This is a common occurrence for campaigns—many a romance novel could be written on these kinds of love stories.)

My story was a little different. Over the course of a year, I began an on-again, off-again fling with a coworker whom I fell in love with in spite of myself, mistaking proximity and intimacy for something real.

In the on-periods of the fling, his company made work genuinely fun. We'd chat during meetings, eat lunch together most days, celebrate birthdays for each other, and spend many nights-turned-into-mornings together, casually greeting each other (again) at the office. When I had a breakdown after a particularly tough round of feedback, he was the one who pushed the hair out of my teary eyes, ordered me two glasses of wine, and gave me a ninety-minute soliloquy on why the feedback was misplaced, in a way only someone who lived and breathed work like I did could have done.

In the off-periods of our fling, work went from hard to being the seventh level of hell. We'd scream at each other at three in the morning then have to sit in meetings together the next day, where I'd bury myself even more into my job to distract from my sadness. After both the campaign and our whatever-it-was-relationship came to a close, I wasn't sure where the grief from the Election Day loss ended and my heartbreak over him began.

Grieving is the only way to describe the period after Election Day. It felt like someone we loved had died. I was at the Javits Center in New York until nearly four in the morning that night and took a cab home from Times Square with a friend. We both sobbed, shaking. I had to pull over in the neighborhood near my home to puke because I just couldn't keep it in anymore.

The next day, in my Hillary sweatshirt, eyes swollen, barely having slept a wink, I went to the concession speech where the only dry eyes in the room were Hillary's. At the lunch we had after, I couldn't handle the flood of emotions, so I tried hard to make people laugh by noting that, hey, since none of us are going to work in government for the next four years, we can all start smoking weed again. At least we'll be high while we mourn.

The weeks after Election Day are a blur. I was numb from sadness. I woke up anxious every morning and instinctively reached for my phone to look at my email, only to see an empty inbox. Six months later, as of the writing of this book, I am still tired. (I am tired in my bones, I am tired in my heart, I am tired even as I sleep eight hours a night. I am genuinely concerned I might always be tired.)

The only thing that kept us all afloat was each other. My campaign family are the only ones who understand what it means to sacrifice like we did. They're the best, the brightest, the most passionate people I'll ever know, and over two years, we worked, mourned, drank, loved and lost together. Now, we'd do anything for each other.

To me, a different career path seems utterly ridiculous. I don't know an alternative way of life other than the certainty that every other year, I will be unemployed on Thanksgiving. It seems bizarre to have "work friends" that are not also "real friends." When I'm on a campaign, every day I *get* to wake up and go to sleep thinking about my mission: To elect a person who shares my beliefs and who can *do* something about it. I have a reason to get out of bed every day!

I have friends who worked on campaigns and then took jobs where they could leave the office at eight or nine instead of midnight. They'd come join us for the final few weeks of the cycle, acting as "campaign tourists," taking on work from those of us who were barely holding it together. They'd watch us drag our exhausted bodies through the office from one meeting to the next with a look of part relief, part envy. "Thank God I left this shit," they'd say. "But, fuck, I do kind of miss this."

I know that what I just described might sound horrible. If you have a family, or want to balance your "life" with your job, it might not be for you. But if you crave community, purpose, and a structure within which you can thrive; if you're willing to work hard and play the game; if you want to be a part of something bigger than yourself; if you want to matter—if you want to know the true limits of your own potential, then work on a campaign.

You'll rediscover that old collegiate feeling of being surrounded by people who are their own special brand of crazy, just like you. Not all campaigns are like presidentials (most aren't, really), but all will take from you as much as you're willing to give and will give you incredible professional mobility. If you're good at what you do and willing to swallow your ego, you'll rise through the ranks quickly.

It is not for the faint of heart, nor for someone who likes life to be easy and predictable. But I promise you: If you work on a campaign, for all of the pain and the sacrifices, you can and will change the world, grow as a professional, and come away with a family you choose.

Campaigns Will Change Your Life

by Marlon Marshall

Director of State Campaigns and Political Engagement for Hillary Clinton's
2016 presidential campaign | Deputy National Field Director for
Barack Obama's 2012 presidential campaign

Campaigns. They will change your life. They're full of many emotions: happiness, joy, pain, sadness, love, and a host of others. You will work many, many, many hours a day with little sleep, wondering how can you make it another year, or another six months, or even another few weeks. You will meet people who will become a part of your community forever. And, like me, you could meet your best friend and end up marrying him or her.

People always ask me, How does one get involved in a campaign? And, more important, why should someone? For me, if you want to make change in this country, it means you need elected officials at all levels of government who share your values. And those values are connected to your personal story—that story that tells others why you care and that you want to do something about it.

As a young child, I saw firsthand the systemic racial inequalities that permeated the St. Louis region. My mother taught fifth grade at a significantly under-resourced school in a predominantly African American neighborhood. She bought pens and pencils for her students—meanwhile, my school roughly ten miles away had the newest computers and technology. That wasn't right! The system was broken for people of color and sadly, in many cases, continues to be.

When you realize the system is broken, you realize one way to strive to fix it is to get on the inside and change it. Systemic racism to this day still plagues this country. Even with this truth, there has been some change and it will only continue if we get people to run for office, work on campaigns, and take charge in their communities. Each day we are starting to see more people run for office who look like the communities they represent, and that is many steps in the right direction.

For me personally, I knew my best route to effect change was to help elect people who shared my values. When I was in college, I served as student body vice president, and I created an action committee of students, faculty, and administrators focused on the recruitment and retention of students of color at the University of Kansas. I learned how to build and organize coalitions and how to use my personal story at the university to help others understand why diversity is important. It was this experience that drew me to campaigns and solidified my decision to change my major. I'll never forget calling my mom to discuss switching from engineering to communications. After spending some time wondering what was wrong with me, she totally had my back, and from there I had to research and learn just how to do this campaign stuff.

What did I do? I volunteered. I had a friend running for state representative, so I canvassed for him. I LOVED it. Getting a chance to talk to people about the community, having conversations about issues they cared about and that I cared about . . . it broke down the barriers that hold us apart as a country. Even when I disagreed with the voter, we understood where the other was coming from. It solidified everything I thought—that I wanted to do this campaign stuff full-time.

Not long after that, I got my first full-time campaign job as an organizer for John Kerry in Kansas City, Missouri. For the first couple of weeks on the job, I hated it. We would work from 9 a.m. until 9 p.m. (at the earliest), calling people to come volunteer for the campaign. I no longer had a personal life, as everything was all about work. I would get home exhausted, with just enough time to eat something quickly, fall asleep, and do it all over again. I forgot to call my family and friends and let them know how I was doing, so then they became worried about me, wondering if everything was okay. I wondered: Is this really for me?

And then I realized: This is the best thing to ever happen to me. What makes you realize that? Volunteers start coming into the office. You see them work as many hours as they can each week, giving their time to the cause to help elect a candidate and create change. I'll never forget Barbara Hershey, a precinct captain in 2004 in Kansas City, Missouri. She wanted to win that election badly and did everything she could to organize her neighborhood on behalf of John Kerry. Her passion to change her community gave me energy each day. I realized that I was coming to work for Barbara, and for the other precinct captains and volunteers, so I could do my part to help them change our communities.

You realize you are learning skills that are integral for any occupation you might ever encounter. You learn how to organize your time. I couldn't manage my own time to save my life before campaigns, and now I have systems that I use in my professional life that help me on the personal side. You learn how to organize people. When people know *why* you're doing what you're doing and what values you have, it makes all the difference. Organizing on campaigns teaches you skills you didn't know you needed.

Lastly, you realize you are creating a new family of sorts—one where the staff works hours on end, and each person has their personal reasons for doing so. You learn about your colleagues' personal stories, what makes them tick, and that everyone has a different experience but is coming together for one common goal—to elect candidates who they believe can make that change. You create a whole new community—people who are there for you during the highest of highs and the lowest of lows. And again, you can meet your lifelong partner. My wife, Stacy, walked into the campaign office in 2004 as a new staffer, and I was the first person she met. Ten years later, we married one another, with friends and family from our campaign community in attendance.

Have I convinced you? Good. Now it's time to get a job. The first thing you should do is find candidates whom you are passionate about and figure out how to volunteer on their campaign. Next, build relationships. Meet with those running the campaign. Ask them how they got to where they did. Pick their brains. Who else can they have you meet with? It's a small network of people who have worked on campaigns and you want to get into this network. And then there are resources such as Democratic Gain, a website where you can find opportunities.

If you're like me and running for office isn't what you envisioned but you want to make change in your own right, help get the people who are running into office. Make that change from the inside. Find people who share your values and get them into office. You will hate it. You will love it. You will meet people who will be a part of your life forever and who will always have your back. And you'll do your part in continuing to move your community and this country forward.

Why haven't you signed up yet?

Politics Isn't Broken

by Teddy Goff

Partner at Precision Strategies | Senior Advisor for Digital and Technology
for Hillary for America | Digital Director of Obama for America

■ **A lot of people will** never forget November 9, 2016, the day after the presidential election. Neither will I, but not for the same reasons.

I spent an hour or two of that day cooped up in a too-small room with the Clinton campaign tech team, a group of fifty or sixty engineers and product managers and designers, most of whom had come to the campaign from companies like Google and Facebook, almost all of whom would have gone back there had we won. But we lost.

Of course, the people gathered were stunned and horrified at what had happened, many openly weeping through the session. But there was also an almost indescribable sense of resolve in that room, and of camaraderie. One by one, they announced that they couldn't imagine going back to a job outside of politics, or activism and advocacy more broadly. They talked about how the campaign had changed them forever. One person disclosed to the group that he had been abused as a child, and said he wanted to devote himself to supporting fellow abuse survivors. Several decided on the spot to launch new ventures together, to harness technology to solve social problems or help people organize in opposition to our new president. Many told moving stories about each other, and the quietly heroic feats they'd seen each other perform over our eighteen-month journey. A few said, to my shock, that they couldn't wait to apply to work on a 2020 presidential campaign.

No one had asked them to keep their messages upbeat. I'd assumed people would be quietly morose or perhaps glib or, worse, accusatory. But the experience of having worked so hard for something so meaningful—and, yes, even the trauma of failing—had ennobled and uplifted them despite their despair.

There were difficult days to follow. But what I remember most about November 9 is the joy in that room.

I've worked on three presidential campaigns and a handful of statewide and municipal races over the past ten years. I am often asked why I've stuck with it. Friends of mine in the tech or media or creative worlds find politics an ugly business, corrupting all who enter it, irrevocably poisoning them with partisanship. Politics is broken, they say.

Here's what I say back: the claim that "politics is broken" is a weapon wielded by the very people trying to break politics—people who've realized that they can create up to 100 percent of the problem but, in our two-party system, incur only 50 percent of the blame if they successfully cast *all politics*, rather than *some politicians*, as awful. And everyone who falls for it—who grows cynical of politics; who starts to believe the two parties aren't all that dissimilar or that everyone who runs for office must have an impure motive; who looks at Washington today and thinks, *ugh, who wants to have anything to do with THAT?*—is an unwitting accomplice to their underlying agenda, which is to weaken and ultimately destroy government by discrediting the system that attracts good people into government in the first place.

I've spent a lot of time with grassroots volunteers in the Democratic Party, and I've had the privilege of spending some time with the highest-ranking Democratic leaders too. Nobody's perfect, but all of them, without a single exception I can think of, got into this line of work and stayed in it because they want to help people. Make health care universal. Do something about climate change and income inequality. Eliminate the cruelties in our criminal justice system. Fix our schools. Rebuild our infrastructure. Reform our immigration laws. Fight for reproductive justice. Make the world safer.

It's hard, often frustrating work. There's nothing glamorous about data entry, or night after night spent calling undecided voters who don't really want to hear from you. Competition can have its pleasures, but in the end there's not a lot of fun in fighting against a party that's dedicated itself to hurting the very people you've dedicated yourself to helping.

But the amazing fact is, despite the slowness, the setbacks, and the transparent ugliness of the process, we often get to accomplish what we set out to do.

Politics is the vehicle by which the Paris Agreement was enacted, marijuana legalized or decriminalized in a growing number of states, health coverage expanded, same-sex marriage legalized. Politics is why we have Social Security and Medicare, and the Civil Rights Act, and women's suffrage, and the First Amendment. The joy of those achievements wasn't just felt by their direct beneficiaries, nor is the credit due just to the presidents and judges who signed their names to them. It is due to the often-anonymous activists who fought for them—sometimes decades or even centuries before they happened—and to the voters who demanded them, and the campaign workers who swung elections in their favor. And, yes, credit is even due to the campaign workers who tried and failed to swing elections, but paved the way for their successors to achieve what they could not.

None of these victories was comprehensive—indeed, many have been or are at risk of being rolled back—and I make no excuse for the gains yet to be made, the injustices that held for far too long, or the abhorrent laws that have been passed alongside the good ones. Those, too, are the product of politics. That's part of why politics needs people like you: you only win if you outnumber the other guys, and keep fighting even after you lose.

But wait, you may be thinking. *Sure, it's better than the alternative, but the Democratic Party also kind of sucks! Why did so many Democrats support the Iraq War and endless drone strikes and surveillance? Why do they give Israel a pass on anything it chooses to do, or cater to their corporate donors? Why haven't they raised the minimum wage, or passed Medicare for all, or made college and housing more affordable?*

Good questions. And they, too, are why you should get into politics.

12

HOW TO ACTUALLY GET A JOB ON A POLITICAL CAMPAIGN

■ **The first thing you need to know** about getting a job on a campaign is that there is no one way to get a job on a campaign.

Campaign organizational structures are often complicated bureaucracies. The smaller the race, the fewer positions a candidate both needs and can afford. Statewide races might have a few hundred employees. Presidential campaigns can employ upward of thousands of people.

The terms you need to know:

- Organizer: Coordinate volunteers and handle voter contact

- Communications: Deal with campaign message and the press

- Digital: Work with social media, the website, graphic design, emails, and videos

- Finance: Raise money

- Political: Deal with allied groups and elected officials

- Research: Know the facts on the candidate and opponent; dig up the dirt

- Advance: Set up and facilitate events

- Operations: Budgets and logistics

- Voter protection: Lawyers who deal with poll watchers and local election administrators

" I like to joke that I grew up as a black lesbian in Scottsdale, Arizona, so how could I not be political? Being aware of current events from a young age was a gateway for being involved in politics, and my personal experience made me understand I had to be involved. The hardest part of my first campaign was the pay. I made $1,500 per month. My mom thought I was crazy taking a job that basically paid me less than minimum wage. Due to the nature of my job as an organizer, it required me to get a car, so I had to lease a car because I didn't have one. I racked up a bunch of credit card debt just to live. One thing I have always tried to do as I attained positions where I could hire staff was to be there for field organizers who, like me, struggled to pay the bills that first cycle and didn't have someone else helping them out financially. A significant part of our lack of diversity on campaigns is about who can afford to drop everything, buy a car, and head to an unknown state to make minimum wage."

—BRYNNE CRAIG, Senior Advisor to the President, Everytown for Gun Safety (2017), National Deputy Director of State Campaigns and Political Engagement for Hillary for America, (2016), Political Director for Terry McAuliffe (2013), and National Field Director at the DCCC (2011–13) on her first job in politics

Here are a few examples of how this might look:

SCHOOL BOARD RACE

Candidate → volunteer treasurer; volunteer campaign manager

STATE SENATE RACE

Candidate → Campaign manager → Finance director (finance assistant), Communications director (communications assistant); Organizing director

GOVERNOR'S RACE IN A BIG STATE

Candidate → Campaign manager → Deputy campaign manager → Finance director (deputy finance director, two finance assistants); political director (three regional political directors, women's vote director, African American vote director, Latino vote director); organizing director (three deputy organizing directors, eight regional organizing directors, seventy-five field organizers, one data director, two deputy data directors, five data assistants); communications director (deputy communications director, rapid response director, press secretary, two communications assistants); research director (research assistant); digital director (deputy digital director, social media manager, digital organizer); policy director (policy assistant); operations director (operations assistant); scheduler (scheduling assistant); advance director (advance associates) GOTV director (GOTV deputy director); voter protection director (three regional voter protection directors)

PRESIDENTIAL CAMPAIGNS

Presidential campaigns are their own clusterfucks so I'm not going to pretend to try to draw it out. There is no one way to structure a presidential campaign, but in general, headquarters will have a full, expansive staff, and then states will have analogous structures to focus on the local intricacies of any given place.

Everything is subject to change.

This is all at the whim of the campaign manager and candidate, who can structure a campaign however they want and can adjust staffing ratios based on what they think they need. They could make up new positions or cut departments entirely. This doesn't include the web of consultants that also make up campaign ecosystems; often, because building in-house teams is too expensive and the skills are too specialized, campaigns will bring on consulting firms to handle all kinds of projects, like advertising (both TV and digital ads), direct mail, polling, research, analytics, digital fundraising, and broader finance needs like telemarketing. On smaller races, lawyers tend to be on retainer but are not actually part of the campaign staff.

Some campaigns and political organizations will hire paid canvassers, who will get paid hourly rates to knock on doors on behalf of the organization.

Finally, the committees and allied groups will hire staff to supplement races, and often the committee and/or state party will actually be the ones employing and organizing staff, because they'll be running coordinated campaigns.

This doesn't include all the volunteer positions, like campaign chair, political advisory board members, finance committees, members of local organizing teams, and "advisors" who take titles to claim credit when the campaigns are over.

■ **Coordinated campaigns:** When multiple candidates for different levels of government are running in the same area on the same ticket, they'll pool resources and work together with coordinated strategy. (This is idealistic, but often it's messy and people's egos get in the way.) The state party might hire a coordinated campaign director, whose job it is to oversee all the races and make sure they play nice. They'll be responsible for ensuring that all candidates in a district are, say, listed on the literature every race is giving out, or that all the field organizers are using the same script for canvasses that lists every candidate, or that canvass universes aren't overlapping. Coordinated campaigns are really important and are also fucking nightmares.

Manage your own expectations. It is rare to join a campaign as a senior staffer without having previous campaign experience. Even if you've got a master's degree or decades of experience in the private sector, you'll probably start as a junior staffer on a campaign unless you've got personal ties to the candidate.

> ■ **Senior staff:** Campaign leadership. Usually defined by the word "director" in their title.

HOW TO FIND CAMPAIGN JOBS

On the progressive side, there are a bunch of listservs you can join to get access to campaign job listings. Do a quick search . . .

> **LEARN MORE ON THE INTERNET** Google "[YOUR PARTY]"
> + "campaign jobs."

On the progressive side, you'll find sites for organizations like Democratic GAIN, Wellstone, Jobs That Are Left, and others. Committees tend to have job banks, as do consulting firms.

For organizing jobs: Check the state party website and the committees. They're usually the ones hiring organizers since it makes more sense for organizing programs to be run out of the coordinated committee.

For specialized skill sets (like digital or communications): Often, the consulting firms are the ones helping source talent for the campaign. If you get in front of the right people at those firms, you'll be part of their talent pool when they need to fill races.

Your best bet is to start by volunteering or interning. I know that's an annoying recommendation. After all, you need a full-time paying job—you can't do shit for free—and it's problematic that people need to start by working for no money in order to eventually get paid because that inherently limits the pool of people who are able to get jobs on campaigns. I don't have an easy solution for this—I wish I could say campaigns should pay interns, but the truth is, there are

199

always people who will do the work for free, so beyond trying to live our values, there isn't a great economic reason to do it.

If a campaign posts an internship and you can swing it, apply for it.

If you get an interview, whether it's for a staff position or an internship, remember that along with brains and the skills laid out in the job description, most campaign staff are looking for two key attributes in new employees or interns:

- A work ethic. You need to show you're willing to work hard. No task is too small for you. You should be ready to give up nights and weekends, and be okay doing mundane, seemingly menial labor. Do not say "no" to any project or assignment, even if it seems beneath you. You want to be a part of the campaign? You'll do whatever it takes.

- Passion. Have a really good reason why you want to work for that specific candidate and why you care about that race. Just like the candidates, you need to identify why you're willing to make sacrifices for this.

If you get hired, keep in mind that your next job will likely come because of someone you work with now. Walk the line between being friendly and being a suck-up. Make your boss's job easier and make them look good—wherever they go next, you want them to have a positive association with you so they bring you along. Try to be a damn delight to work with. The intern you work with one cycle could be your peer the next cycle and hiring people the cycle after that, so don't ever treat someone as beneath you.

13
PHONE CALLS AND TWEETING AND MARCHING, OH MY
(OR, ACTIVISM 101)

■ **Outside of campaigns,** there are ways you can hold your elected officials accountable and make them earn your vote. Making phone calls, tweeting, emailing, writing letters, and showing up at town halls or public forums to ask questions are all various ways to show that you're paying attention and that you have a position you expect them to represent.

There are great groups to help you identify who to target and how to target them, and to plug you in with other volunteers who want to keep sustained pressure on your leadership. If you're a progressive like me, check out Indivisible, Organizing for Action, or Our Revolution. There are Facebook groups you can join and email lists to sign up for that will send you daily actions you can take to #resist Trump.

Sign up for emails from these groups, go to their events, make those calls, and get involved if you want to. March at protests, share photos on Facebook, save your elected officials' numbers in your phone and make sure they hear from you daily. None of it will hurt the cause and it will be a great way to meet interesting people.

But, in the spirit of this book, a little real talk: The reason an elected official cares that you're paying attention is because of the impact it might have on their reelection. It all comes back to their own job security. If activists draw attention to the bad things the elected official is doing, their voters (and donors) might notice.

So if you really want to hold an elected official you don't like accountable, don't forget two key actions: Donate to their opponent and vote against them when you can.

Nothing scares an elected official more than a well-funded opponent. Calls to their office and floods of people at their town hall work because these are symbols of an opposition that is fired up and willing to put their money and time on the line. Take it to the logical next level. If your member of Congress isn't doing what you want, go help their opponent. Then tweet or post on Facebook about it and encourage your friends to do the same.

Then, dear God, for the love of all that is holy and righteous, please vote.

I shouldn't have to ask you. I hope that if you're holding this book in your hands (or on your e-reader, or whatever), that you're a registered voter and you vote in every single election.

But probability means you likely don't vote every single time you get a chance to. Maybe you didn't vote by absentee ballot in college, or maybe you missed the local elections. Or maybe you're not even registered yet!

Fix that. I can't believe I even have to argue this after the consequences of the 2016 election, but just in case, let me be explicit: Voting is your civic duty, your right, responsibility, and your privilege.

People will tell you that you can't complain if you don't vote. Those people may be self-righteous but they're not wrong. Complaints are meaningless if you don't follow them up with action.

If you don't like any of the candidates, well, those are your choices. Suck it up and cast your ballot anyway for the good of your community, because your vote doesn't just affect you—it affects your town, your state, and your country. Put your self-interest aside and think of the more vulnerable around you. Which candidate will do more for the people who have the least?

Don't presume that a politician has to inspire you in order for you to show up. Yes, politicians should, in an ideal world, make a compelling case to you, the voter, as to why they deserve your trust and respect. (That's literally what I've been arguing for the last 200-ish pages; I hope any candidate who uses this book to run for office does exactly that.)

But not voting doesn't punish those candidates or teach them a lesson. Fewer people voting doesn't mean that no one wins—it just means that YOU lose because you didn't have a say and now you're stuck with whoever everyone else chose. To borrow the cliché, decisions are made by those who show up. Want a politician who will cater to your interests? Become a voter they can count on.

> ■ Genuinely hate all the candidates? Cast your vote anyway, and then next cycle, run yourself, or recruit a friend you like to run, or join your local political party and see if you can help push them to find candidates that better suit your interests. Quit your bitching and fix the problem yourself.

Get engaged, stay engaged, and don't stop doing it just because you don't win every fight (or it doesn't make for good Instagrams). Participating in democracy is part of being a good citizen and ultimately, part of being a good person.

CONCLUSION

■ **In the introduction,** I argue that running for office is really fucking hard.

And it is—it requires time, energy, and sacrifice. There are no shortcuts to winning an election. You've got to be willing to humble yourself for your constituents. You work for the people, not the other way around.

But when you boil it down, being a candidate (and then, an elected official) is actually relatively simple. Decide what you believe, then articulate those beliefs to genuinely connect with voters. Be real with them—show vulnerability by putting your heart and passion on display. Be honest, kind, and grateful. Be a good person like your mother raised you to be, and try to do it all with a sense of humor.

It's certainly scary. Anytime you take a stand, someone somewhere is going to disagree with you and tell you you're wrong. You're going to have to defend your principles, and you'll be held accountable for the choices you make.

But you will change the world. Win or lose, by running, you're going to inspire people to take action too. You're going to show them that "real people" can take charge of our government, not just as voters but as leaders.

If you decide to run for office, sign up at runforsomething.net—we will help you. (I promise!) We exist to support young people running for local office for the first or second time. We'll walk you through the steps, find you mentors, and maybe even give you money.

And if you decide not to run, you can sign up at runforsomething.net too. Help other people run for the first time. Chip in if you can, or volunteer, or find a candidate in your community and go knock on doors with him or her.

Whatever you decide to do, and however you decide to get involved, I hope you take the following sentence to heart:

Stop fucking complaining and do something.

We're in a new era of American politics; we're all a little tired and a little broken. It's hard to watch the news every day or to sit in front of Facebook or Twitter and refresh to get the latest bullshit. Each *New York Times* notification on my phone makes me cringe. I get why you might say "fuck it" and switch to HGTV. (I watch HGTV all day in the background while I work; 24-7 news channels have no place in my home.)

It's tempting to relieve yourself of the burden to solve the problem because complaining is both easy and cathartic. It is so much harder to actually try to fix the system, and it requires some swallowing of your own ego, because you might fail. But you have to try. There is no alternative.

During the 2016 presidential campaign, one of my best friends/coworkers and I used to joke around that the way we knew we were deeply burned out was that we had started to find inspirational sayings genuinely moving. "You know, you miss 100 percent of the shots you never take," he'd say to me. "Reach for the moon and you'll land among the stars," I'd retort.

Never one to be sucked in by cheesy sayings, by the end of the election, I was so tired and so drained that I found myself repeating as a mantra the same ethos Hillary laid out as her guiding compass: "Do all the good you can."

It's not "talk about doing all the good," nor is it "tweet about doing all the good," nor even "support others who do all the good," although that's important too.

It's "DO."

Do. March. Run! I promise. You can do it. We'll help.

APPENDIX

Absentee vote: A ballot cast before Election Day because the voter can't make it in person. Some states have no-excuse absentee voting (meaning, anyone can request and return a ballot); other states have stringent rules about what counts as a reason for not being able to vote on Election Day.

ActBlue: An online donation platform that helps Democrats and progressive causes raise money. Learn more at ActBlue.com.

Action Network: An online platform for progressives that enables organizing through mass email, events, petitions, and other tools. Learn more at actionnetwork.org.

Alderman: A person who serves on a municipal council or assembly. Often another word for city councilman or city councilwoman.

Annie's List: An organization in Texas that recruits and supports women running for state and local office. There are similar organizations like Annie's List all across the country for specific states—Ruth's List in Florida and Eleanor's Legacy in New York, to start.

Ballotpedia.org: A great website that crowd-sources information about elections and candidates. As reputable as Wikipedia—if you trust Wikipedia, trust Ballotpedia.

BatchGeo: An online tool that lets you take a spreadsheet full of addresses and map them out. Feels like magic!

Bicameral legislature: A legislature with two houses or chambers. Think: Congress, which is made up of the House and the Senate. Nearly every legislature in the United States is bicameral, except for Nebraska.

Blue state (or red state): Shorthand to refer to the way a state usually votes during a presidential election. Blue states give their electoral votes to Democrats; red states give theirs to Republicans.

Blue State Digital: A digital agency that also builds a tool by the same name that lets organizations and campaigns send email, host events, and build an email list. Learn more at bluestatedigital.com.

Camp Wellstone: Paul Wellstone was a senator from Minnesota from 1991 until he died in a plane crash in 2002. He was remarkable for running a true grassroots campaign, driven by young people, people of color, and others who don't usually get involved in politics—he was generally understood to be a very good guy. After his death, folks created Wellstone Action, a nonprofit that trains progressives to run for office. The training programs they run are called Camp Wellstone. Learn more at wellstone.org.

Catalist: A vendor that sells the voter file. Google 'em.

Caucus: A way of holding an election in which, during a single period of time, a bunch of people gather and literally vote with their feet. People who pick candidate A will stand on one side of the room, people who pick candidate B will stand on the other side, and candidate C supporters might stand in the middle. Delegates are then given out proportionally, and if any one candidate doesn't hit a "viability" threshold by reaching a certain amount of support, those supporters must realign to a different side.

Citizens United v. FEC: The Supreme Court decision that allowed for the creation of super PACs, which can raise and spend unlimited money without disclosing who the money comes from.

Collective PAC: A great organization that works to build black political power by supporting black candidates across the country. Go to collectivepac.org for more details.

Constant Contact: An online tool to let corporations and organizations send mass emails.

Cook Partisan Voting Index (PVI): A number calculated by comparing how your district voted relative to the country as a whole during the last two presidential elections. A PVI of "D+5" means that the district's voter spread resulted in an average of five points more Democratic than the national spread.

Cycle: Politics works in two-year "cycles"—kind of like how television runs in seasons. Typically, the odd years are considered "off years" or "out of cycle," and the even years, during which there are federal elections, are "in cycle." Very few states hold statewide elections during the off years; notable exceptions include Virginia and New Jersey.

DailyKos: A progressive group blog of sorts that takes "diaries" from bloggers and organizations all across the country. DailyKos runs a massive email list and raises money for progressive candidates.

Democracy for America (DFA): After his failed presidential campaign in 2004, Howard Dean created DFA to support progressive candidates and issues around the country. DFA asks its members (people on its email list) to vote on its endorsements.

Democratic Congressional Campaign Committee (DCCC or "D-Trip"): The committee that handles House races. The Republican equivalent is the National Republican Congressional Committee (NRCC).

Democratic Governors Association (DGA): The committee that oversees strategy for Democrats in gubernatorial races. The Republican equivalent is the Republican Governors Association (RGA).

Democratic Legislative Campaign Committee (DLCC): The committee that focuses on state House and Senate races. Republicans run this strategy through their Republican Legislative Campaign Committee (RLCC).

Democratic National Committee: The committee in charge of the presidential nominating process, overseeing state parties and coordinating broader Democratic strategy. The Republican version is the Republican National Committee (RNC).

Democratic Senatorial Campaign Committee: The committee that works with Democratic members of the Senate. Republicans, unsurprisingly, call theirs the National Republican Senatorial Committee (NRSC).

Development, Relief, and Education for Alien Minors Act (DREAM Act): Legislation that would give a pathway to citizenship to young people who came to this country as children without documentation. (People eligible for this program are known as Dreamers.) Congress has consistently failed to pass the DREAM Act—as a holdover, in 2012, President Obama created a program called the Deferred Action for Childhood Arrivals (DACA), which allows Dreamers to apply for work permits. Trump has threatened to fuck with DACA on a regular basis.

Direct mail: What a campaign sends you that you probably glance at, let sit on your counter for a few days, then toss in the trash.

Earned media: Stories in the press that the campaign has "earned" coverage of. (Sometimes it really is that simple.)

EMILY's List: A national PAC that supports pro-choice women running for office. Go give them money—emilyslist.org.

Establishment (or party): In this book, those words are used interchangeably to mean the network of organizations, including the Democratic National Committee (DNC), the Democratic Congressional Campaign Committee (DCCC), the Democratic Senatorial Campaign Committee (DSCC), the

Democratic Legislative Campaign Committee (DLCC), the Democratic Governors Association (DGA), the state parties, and all affiliated groups.

General election: An election usually between the two major political parties (and sometimes independents or third party candidates) that determines who will ultimately hold the office up for grabs. A primary is an election between people in the same party, trying to win the party's nomination.

Gerrymandering: The explicit manipulation of boundaries of an electoral jurisdiction in order to favor a party or class. How this works in practice: Partisan leadership will draw new electoral districts in order to make sure all the voters in that district match their partisan leanings.

Get Out the Vote (GOTV): A term used to mean both the stretch of time before Election Day as well as the work done during that period of time to actually get people to cast their ballots.

Grassroots tweeter: A meaningless phrase that campaigns use when what they really mean is "real person who advocates for us on the internet."

Hustle: A new tool that helps campaigns and organizations do one-to-one texting en masse. Go to hustle.com for more information.

Incumbent: The person who holds office.

Independent expenditure: Activity in support of—but independent from—a campaign. In most races (with some variation based on state law), in the weeks or months leading up to Election Day, IE organizations are legally prohibited from coordinating directly with the campaigns they're advocating for. IE work might include advertising or organizing (canvasses or phone banks), or anything else an organization might take on.

Jungle primary: A type of election where the top two finishers go on to the general election, regardless of party. If 10 people run, five Democrats and five Republicans, but the top two finishers are both Democrats, then the general election will consist of two Democrats.

Labor union: A group of organized workers that tends to focus on collective bargaining over wages, benefits, and working conditions in their particular industry. Many unions also get involved in politics as a way of advocating for legislation and policies that benefit their membership.

Latino Victory Project: An organization that works to build Latino political power by supporting Latino candidates. Learn more at latinovictory.us.

Leadership Institute: The conservative training program that's existed since 1979. They have a massive budget to work with conservative candidates, staff, and volunteers. The GOP has been doing this shit for decades—it's part of the reason why they've won so many more down-ballot races than Democrats.

Media market: The region reached by a TV or radio station. For example: The DC media market actually includes people who live as far away as Baltimore or the outer suburbs in Virginia.

MoveOn: A progressive policy group created in 1998 in response to President Bill Clinton's impeachment. They raise money for candidates and advocate for progressive issues. Learn more at moveon.org.

Name ID: Literally how many people recognize your name and have an opinion about you.

NationBuilder: An online tool you can use to send email, take in money, and host events. Learn more at nationbuilder.com.

NGP VAN: A tool Democrats use to organize the voter file and donor information for compliance purposes. Get the details at ngpvan.com.

Organizing for Action: The 501(c)4 organization that President Obama created after his successful reelection campaign. OFA is entirely separate from the DNC, a controversial decision that has given birth to a thousand thinkpieces.

Our Revolution: The 501(c)4 organization that Bernie Sanders created after his failed presidential run in 2016. They support progressive candidates (both Democrats and independents) and do issue advocacy. Learn more at ourrevolution.com.

Overton window: Also known as "the window of discourse," used to describe the range of ideas the public will accept.

Political Action Committee (PAC): An organization that collects money and then donates it to a political cause or candidate. PACs are also called 527s because of the part of the tax code that applies to them.

Progressives: There are a lot of definitions of "progressives"—to be clear, when I use it, I'm describing people who are prochoice, who care about equality, tolerance, inclusion, reducing income inequality, preventing gun violence, combatting climate change, fighting for immigrants' rights, health care for all—people who are pro-facts and pro–voting rights.

Progressive Change Campaign Committee (PCCC): A candidate training and grassroots advocacy group that considers themselves to be the official arm of the "Elizabeth Warren wing" of the Democratic party. Learn more at boldprogressives.org.

***Reynolds v. Sims*:** The Supreme Court decision from 1964 that ruled that state legislature districts must be equal in size (unlike the U.S. Senate, in which a senator from Wyoming represents substantially fewer people than a senator from New York). This forced state legislatures across the country to redraw their districts and requires regular revision.

Robocall: An automated phone call you might get from a campaign. Pretty annoying; marginally effective.

Romneycare: Before there was Obamacare, there was Romneycare—as Governor of Massachusetts, Mitt Romney passed health care reform in

Massachusetts to provide affordable coverage to his state's residents. It wasn't perfect, but it provided a model on which to base Obamacare.

Shift: A term campaigns use to mean a block of time they're scheduling volunteers. A shift might last for one hour, or it might last for three.

Special interest: An umbrella term used to mean anything from an advocacy group to a lobbying organization. Some special-interest groups are extraordinarily powerful and can mobilize massive amounts of money and volunteers when they get involved (think: the NRA on the right and Planned Parenthood on the left).

Super PAC: An independent-expenditure-only committee that can raise and spend unlimited amounts of money but cannot directly donate to or coordinate with a campaign.

Tables: In politics, this refers to groups of organizations or donors who coordinate strategy or, more often, money.

Turnout: A percentage used to measure how many people actually show up at the polls. Divide the number of people who voted by the number of people who are registered to vote in any particular jurisdiction. Multiply that by 100 and you'll get your turnout.

Uncontested election: When there is only one candidate running in any single race. Utter bullshit.

Voter file: The voter file is a list of registered voters, including their name, address, history of voting behavior, and as much information as possible.

Win number: The number of votes you'll likely need to win. In most races, that number is often called your "50+1", meaning 50 percent of the votes cast plus one to get you the majority.

ACKNOWLEDGMENTS

■ **The year 2017 has been really fucking hard.** Outside of the election and the emotional wreckage in its wake, I spent much of the first four months of the year on crutches recovering from a traumatic knee injury and then from reconstructive surgery. Two things (outside of my monster dog, of course) saved me from falling too deep into a dark place:

1. Run for Something (both the organization and this book). I threw myself 200 percent into this work. This has been the best possible coping mechanism.

2. I've somehow lucked into having the best friends, family, and friends-turned-family imaginable. I can't possibly name each and every person who helped me over the last year. (But I am going to try!)

First, thanks to my agent, Stephanie Delman at Greenburger Associates, who slid into my Twitter DMs and changed my life. (The only time I've ever been glad to have open DMs.) Her kindness, passion for the work we're doing, and her patience with me as I asked for explanations through every step of the publishing process are why the thing you're holding exists.

Second, thank you to Jhanteigh Kupihea, a staggeringly good person and a great editor whose feedback was invaluable and who understood from day one what I wanted to accomplish with this book.

J & S, thank you both for answering my crazy emails, for being eager audiences for anecdotes from my weird-as-hell life, and for regularly reminding me that I'm qualified to write this book simply by being the one doing it. You two should both run for office.

Thank you to the rest of the folks at Atria Books and Simon & Schuster. Publisher Judith Curr has been a champion for this book from day one, and I'm so glad to have Ariele Fredman as my publicist, a woman who immediately picked up what I was throwing down. Thank you, too, to Sarah Wright, Dana Sloan, Albert Tang, Kimberly Goldstein, Polly Watson, the legal team, the marketing team, and Scott Kaufman and Hadley Walker at the Simon & Schuster Speakers Bureau, all of whom handled me with grace and patience. Every single one of you should run for office too.

(Assume from here on out that nearly every person I mention should run for office. They'd all be great.)

Jennifer Kinon and Scott Hill from the Original Champions of Design took my "it should be more, I don't know, fresh?" gibberish feedback and turned it into this stunning book and cover. Victor Ng took the photo of me, which only took four months for me to come to tolerate. (Sadie makes it acceptable.)

Thanks to Lily Weber and Cassandra Marketos for doing many of the interviews found in this book and helping push the RFS #content train forward.

Thank you so much to all my contributors: Senator Cory Booker, Emmy Ruiz, Jen O'Malley Dillon, Addisu Demissie, Brynne Craig, Marlon Marshall, John Podesta, Robby Mook, Jason Kander, Pete Buttigieg, Stacey Abrams, Andrew Gillum, Will Guzzardi, Nelson Roman, Liz Doerr, Eric Lesser, Svante Myrick, Darrin Camilleri, Caroline Simmons, and Chaz Beasley. Kudos to Sommer Omar, Jeff Giertz, and Abe Rakov for making some of those contributions possible as well.

Thank you to Huma Abedin, Nick Merrill, and Lauren Peterson for enabling Hillary Clinton's contribution to this book. And thank you to Secretary Clinton—I can't begin to express gratitude for everything you've done for me personally and for our work, but I'll start with a simple thank-you for modeling the kind of tenacity and grit I try to emulate every day. You should be president.

Patrick Stevenson, Alex Wall, Danielle Kantor, Danielle Butterfield, and Ezra

Mechaber: Thank you. I know this has not been a stellar year to have me as a friend—between the work, the book, the broken knee, and the sadness, I have been absent more often than not. You each dragged me out of my self-imposed isolation, made me laugh, helped me write, gut-checked my crazy, consoled me when I was broken, inspired me, grounded me, and made sure my monster-dog was never abandoned. There is no group of people I'd rather go through hell with. I'm so very sorry you've had to put up with me this year, and forever grateful that you all did.

I am a shell of a human without my various groups of girlfriends—Liz Zaretsky, Amy Beihl, Taylor Salditch, Nichole Sessego, Jenna Lowenstein, Jess Morales Rocketto, and Katie Dowd—and my Island Times Strategies soulmates, Caitlin Mitchell, Martha Patzer, and Sarah Driscoll. Thank you for the drinks, the various group threads, the adventures, the feedback on this book, and literally everything else, and for helping me shine by shining even brighter yourselves. Please all run for office, then if you have the time, please takeover the world.

I'm prouder than ever to be a part of the HFA family, who I had the utter delight to work hard, play hard, and make history with. I wish I could list all your names—you will never get the credit you deserve for the innovative and jaw-droppingly good work you did. The HFA email team in particular were the reasons I got out of bed every morning for two years, God bless them.

A special thank-you to Christina Reynolds, whose feedback on this book and most other things has made me smarter, better, and bolder. Reynolds, I'm so lucky to have you in my corner.

R, 2016 was often harder because of you, but just as often (if not more so), you made it all so much better. Thank you for reading this book and for your unwavering confidence in what I might be capable of, even through all our bullshit.

The Florida 2014 team went through a true shitstorm together—our two-years-and-counting ongoing group text continues to make my day. In particular, thank you to Greg Goddard and Brendan Gilfillan, who both helped me refine RFS in the early days and continue to look out for me.

I got my first taste of what a campaign family can be in 2012 and at Organizing for Action. Nearly everyone I worked with over the first three years of my career took me under their collective wing and taught me how to be a grown-up in this world. I would be remiss not to thank Toby and Laura Fallsgraff, Nate Lubin, and Dan Scarvalone for standing by me.

Teddy Goff, you've hired me for nearly every job I've had, and I am who I am professionally because for some reason, you kept giving me a chance. (Sorry, dude, but it's true.) Thanks for both keeping me humble and pushing me to be better.

J. D. Bryant, my sunshine—you don't just give me permission to be my truest, kookiest, best and worst self; you demand it of me and you love me for it. The feeling is mutual.

Thank you to my few but mighty "real people" friends—Sarah Eberspacher, Ashley Greene, Mimi Stein, and Mike Deem—for reminding me that there's a world outside this bubble and it's not all bad.

My "just *do* something" attitude comes from my parents, Richard and Cheryl— my siblings, Jessi, Daniel (aka Bonnie X Clyde, Google it, seriously) and Vicky are living proof that it runs in the gene pool. Thanks, Mom and Dad, for not asking (too many) questions when I turned down jobs in January because I wanted to give this thing a shot. You gave me the tools to succeed but just as importantly, the permission to fail.

Ninety percent of what I do with my life is done explicitly to make my grandparents proud. (The other 10 percent of what I do, I hope they never find out about.) Elliot Goldstein and Sharla and Frank Neuberger, thanks for being my number one fans and I'm sorry for cursing so much.

The Run for Something team stuns me with their capacity for work, for doing good, and for creativity and scrappiness. A special shout out to my cofounder and partner-in-not-quite-crime, Ross Morales Rocketto, and a triple-exclamation-mark thank-you (!!!) to Seisei Tatebe-Goddu, Sarah Horvitz, Bridget Siegel, Dara Freed, Brian Zuzenak, Catherine Gabel, Eduardo Silva, Pete Gibson, and Graham Wilson.

A monumental thank-you to the HFA and OFA folks who've helped with RFS in ways big and small, including Yahel Carmon, Nat Thompson, Derek Parham, Jacob Leibenluft, Jesse Ferguson, Thea Raymond Sidel, Deepa Subramaniam, Julie Zuckerbrod, Natasha Lawrence, Tyrone Gayle, Ian Sams, Jennifer Palmieri, Debra Cohen and so many others who answered my questions, read early Google Docs, introduced me to others, walked my dog, reviewed budgets, and did any number of things to help make this organization a reality.

Those people, along with wonderful interns, volunteers, and of course, our candidates, are going to change the world. Watch out.

If you've gotten this far, you're probably thinking about running for office or working on a campaign. I hope you do it. Your decision to *do* something about your frustrations and to sacrifice so much to make the world a better place is what makes my work (and the work of so many others) worth it.

You make me feel a little bit better when most things make me feel a little bit worse. Thank you, thank you, thank you.

NOTES

1. Seth Motel, "Who Runs for Office? A Profile of the 2%," *FactTank* (blog), Pew Resarch Foundation, September 3, 2014.

2. Jocelyn Drummond, Qian Zhang, and Victoria Lawson, *Who Runs Our Cities? The Political Gender Gap in the Top 100 U.S. Cities* (New York: CUNY Institute for State and Local Governance), 2016.

3. Claire Cain Miller, "The Problem for Women Is Not Winning. It's Deciding to Run," *New York Times*, October 25, 2016.

4. Philip Bump, "The Unprecedented Partisanship of Congress, Explained," *Washington Post*, January 13, 2016.

5. Chris Lusvardi, "What Election? Majority on Macon County Ballot Uncontested," *Decatur Herald & Review*, March 19, 2017.

6. Donald W. Meyers, "Uncontested School District Races Common in Washington, Yakima County," *Yakima Herald*, January 24, 2017.

7. Naomi Nix, "Welcome to New Jersey, Where More Than Half of All School Board Races Have One—or No—Candidate," *The 74*, March 20, 2016.

8. *The 2016 State of Wisconsin's Cities and Villages* (Madison, WI: League of Wisconsin Municipalities/Wisconsin Taxpayers Alliance), 2016, http://www .lwm-info.org/DocumentCenter/View/809.

9. Alan Greenblatt, "Uncontested Legislative Races Are Becoming More Common," *Governing*, June 2016.

10. Rong-Gong Lin II, "When City Council Elections Are Uncontested, Some Cities Opt to Cancel," *Los Angeles Times*, November 3, 2014.

11. Michael D. Pitman, "State Lawmaker Drafts Bill to Eliminate Unnecessary Elections," *Dayton Daily News*, August 19, 2016.

12. Eric Ostermeier, "1 in 7 US House Races Have Only One Major Party Candidate on November Ballot," *Smart Politics*, September 7, 2016.

13. Heather Caygle, "Sanders-Loving Vermont Lawmaker Snags GOP Nomination," *Politico*, October 7, 2016.

14. Katie Leslie, "Is Dallas Rep. Pete Sessions Vulnerable After Clinton Won His District?" *Dallas News*, December 12, 2016.

15. Carl Klarner, "Democracy in Decline: The Collapse of the 'Close Race' in State Legislatures," *Ballotpedia*, May 6, 2015.

16. David M. Konisky and Michiko Ueda, "The Effects of Uncontested Elections on Legislator Performance," *Legislative Studies Quarterly* 36, no. 2 (May 2011): 199–229.

ABOUT THE AUTHOR

AMANDA LITMAN is the cofounder and executive director of Run for Something, a PAC that helps recruit and support young, diverse progressives running for down-ballot office. Previously, she was the email director for Hillary Clinton's 2016 presidential campaign, digital director for Charlie Crist's 2014 Florida gubernatorial campaign, deputy email director for Organizing for Action, and an email writer for Barack Obama's 2012 reelection campaign. She graduated from Northwestern University in 2012 with a BA in American Studies. She lives in Brooklyn with her rescue dog, Sadie. For more information, visit runforsomething.net and follow @amandalitman on Twitter.